JENNIFER SERRAVALLO

FOREWORD BY Ellin Oliver Keene

The
Literacy Teacher's
Playbook

GRADES 3–6

Four Steps for Turning Assessment Data
into Goal-Directed Instruction

HEINEMANN

Portsmouth, NH

Heinemann
361 Hanover Street
Portsmouth, NH 03801–3912
www.heinemann.com

Offices and agents throughout the world

The author and publisher wish to thank those who have generously given permission to reprint borrowed material:

Figure 1.2: Reading Interest Inventory from "'But There's Nothing Good to Read' (In the Library Media Center)" by Denice Hildebrandt originally appeared in *Media Spectrum: The Journal for Library Media Specialists in Michigan* (vol. 28, no. 3, pp. 34–37, Fall 2001). Reprinted by permission of the author.

Credits continue on page iv.

Library of Congress Cataloging-in-Publication Data
Serravallo, Jennifer.
    The literacy teacher's playbook, grades 3–6 : four steps for turning assessment data into goal-directed instruction / Jennifer Serravallo.
        pages cm
    Includes bibliographical references.
    ISBN-13: 978-0-325-04353-1
    ISBN-10: 0-325-04353-1
    1. Language arts (Elementary)—United States—Evaluation.
LB1576.S343425 2013
372.6—dc23   2013024162

Editors: Kate Montgomery and Zoë Ryder White
Production: Victoria Merecki
Typesetter: Gina Poirier, Gina Poirier Design
Cover and interior designs: Suzanne Heiser
Cover and interior photographs: Michelle Baker and Nick Christoff
Manufacturing: Steve Bernier

Printed in the United States of America on acid-free paper
19   18   17   EBM   3   4   5   6

For Bam and Poppy

Credits continued from page ii:

Figure 1.5: "Running-Record Note-Taking" from *Conferring with Readers: Supporting Each Student's Growth and Independence* by Jennifer Serravallo and Gravity Goldberg. Copyright © 2007 by Jennifer Serravallo and Gravity Goldberg. Published by Heinemann, Portsmouth, NH. All rights reserved.

Figure 1.7: "A Tough Day for Thomas" by Shannon Rigney Keane from The Reading and Writing Project © 2010: http://readingandwritingproject.com/public/themes/rwproject /resources/assessments/additional_tools/tough_day_for_thomas.pdf. Reprinted by permission of Teachers College Reading and Writing Project, Columbia University, New York.

Figures 1.8 and 2.15: Student Response forms from *Independent Reading Assessment: Fiction* by Jennifer Serravallo. Copyright © 2012 by Jennifer Serravallo. Published by Scholastic Inc. Reprinted by permission of the publisher.

Figures 2.7–2.14: Student expectations graphics from *Independent Reading Assessment: Fiction* and *Independent Reading Assessment: Nonfiction* by Jennifer Serravallo. Copyright © 2012 and 2013 by Jennifer Serravallo. Published by Scholastic Inc. Reprinted by permission of the publisher.

Figure 2.16: NAEP fluency scale (2002): https://nces.ed.gov/nationsreportcard/studies /ors/scale.asp. Reprinted by permission of the National Center for Education Statistics, Institute for Education Sciences, U.S. Department of Education.

Figure 4.3: "Three Levels of Decision Making to Move Children Toward Independence" from *Teaching Reading in Small Groups: Differentiated Instruction for Building Strategic, Independent Readers* by Jennifer Serravallo. Copyright © 2010 by Jennifer Serravallo. Published by Heinemann, Portsmouth, NH. All rights reserved.

Figure 4.4: Diagram of gradual release of responsibility from *Better Learning Through Structured Teaching: A Framework for the Gradual Release of Responsibility* by Douglas Fisher and Nancy Frey. Copyright © 2008 by the Association for Supervision and Curriculum Development (ASCD). Reprinted by permission of the Copyright Clearance Center on behalf of ASCD.

Figure 4.8: Class Profile form from *Independent Reading Assessment: Fiction* by Jennifer Serravallo. Copyright © 2012 by Jennifer Serravallo. Published by Scholastic Inc. Reprinted by permission of the publisher.

Figure 4.9: Planning Your Week form from *Independent Reading Assessment: Fiction* by Jennifer Serravallo. Copyright © 2012 by Jennifer Serravallo. Published by Scholastic Inc. Reprinted by permission of the publisher.

Contents

Knowing When the Goal Has Been Met 143

Wrap-Up 145

To download the student writing samples
and reproducible forms featured
throughout this book, please visit
www.heinemann.com/products/E04353.aspx
(click on the Companion Resources tab).

Foreword

I have three questions for you before you plunge into Jen Serravallo's *The Literacy Teacher's Playbook:*

1. Have you lost sleep over your frustration that the literacy assessments you're required to use don't provide specific direction for your instruction?
2. Have you tossed and turned all night worrying about a student? You know there are complex reasons for his or her lack of progress or engagement, but you can't get your arms around what they are.
3. Have you lain awake wondering how to select appropriate literacy goals for children and involve them in meeting these goals?

Then this is your book! It will bring you closer to answers to these questions.

First, you are not alone in your frustration about commonly used literacy assessments. I have had countless conversations with friends outside education about why the assessments on which policymakers ask us to base our decisions about children's lives are at best inadequate. They typically ask what the alternative is, and I tell them we need a wide range of assessment and observation tools in order to fully understand children's strengths and needs. We need formal assessments, yes, but mostly we need a mosaic that includes children's daily work, our observations, children's reflections on their own growth, and metacognitive barometers of engagement and interest. We need a process for describing children's strengths and needs in much greater detail; we need a fuller, more descriptive profile of each child in order to guide her or his learning wisely. Not so easy, right?

The very premise of "a" literacy assessment (even one with several subtests) is flawed. To understand the complex factors that contribute to children's success as readers, writers, speakers, and listeners, we need to study their growth over time in a variety of ways. *The Literacy Teacher's Playbook* introduces a stunning array of tools you can use to gather information that you can—wait for it, this is shocking—use to guide your instruction! In the first chapter, Jen includes "lenses and tools" that will help you get a 360-degree view of your students' strengths and needs. Taken together, these tools eclipse any existing literacy assessments I can name.

Regarding the second question, I still lie awake puzzling over kids and I don't have my own classroom anymore. Part of the worry is that even when we have data, it's very difficult to understand it. We pour through assessment data and look at work samples, but too often we're not sure what the data *show*—what are we to make of all those numbers and piles of work?

Jen provides impeccable guidance on how to analyze and interpret the range of data you've collected. I took Jen's advice and studied Alex's work samples (provided in Appendix A) to see how much I could learn about a child I've never met. It was astonishing. I feel I know this kid, I believe I have some idea about where to begin work with him. I see his strengths and some real patterns of need. Carefully analyzing Alex's work is like staring at one of those drawings in which you cannot see an embedded image until someone helps you perceive it another way. Suddenly, out pops the hidden figure and you can't believe you didn't notice it right away. Wait till you try this process! It will remind you why you went into teaching. Children are complex, endlessly fascinating, and it takes all our intellectual energy to understand them—for teachers, that is pure joy.

Finally, on the question of finding the sweet spot—the goal or direction that will inspire and lead children to new depths in learning—Jen's final chapter is filled with actionable ideas to build instruction on the data you've analyzed and interpreted. She makes clear that "every possible area of growth [for a child] comes from a strength." Jen is suggesting that we build learning goals alongside children and that those goals rest on the most reliable foundation for instruction—trustworthy and multifaceted data. The four-step protocol she suggests ensures that we will have reliable data and know how to act on it.

Reading this book was a joy. It helped me relocate convictions I've long held but that are often obscured by policy and practice challenges. I'm reminded that we can, through good old-fashioned kidwatching and careful analysis of children's behavior and work samples, understand what we need to know about guiding them wisely and helping them find their intellectual power. That is the real joy.

Read this book, put those questions to bed, and start getting some sleep!

Ellin Oliver Keene

Acknowledgments

Gone are the days when teachers would walk into their classroom, close the door, and go about their business. The work it takes to become a great teacher is in large part team-work. And so it is with me, a teacher turned staff developer turned author. Everything has been possible only because of the great teams who support me.

Thanks, first, to the team at the Teachers College Reading and Writing Project (TCRWP). Much of the work described in this book began when I was a senior staff developer at this amazing organization. Thanks especially to the founding director, Lucy Calkins, and senior staff members Kathleen Tolan, Mary Ehrenworth, Amanda Hartman, and Laurie Pessah for your inspiration, encouragement, leadership, knowledge, and generosity. Every member of TCRWP, past and present, has influenced me in immeasurable ways; every Thursday for eight years we met to ask good questions, outgrow our best thinking, and support one another in our own professional development. Specifically, I want to thank Carl Anderson, Mary Chiarella, Donna Santman, Colleen Cruz, Cory Gillette, Brooke Geller, Emily Smith, Elizabeth Moore, Ami Mehta, Joe Yukish, and Alison Porcelli. Your footprints are all over this book.

Thanks as well to the teams of educators with whom I've been lucky enough to learn beside. I have been refining the ideas in this book based on feedback from brilliant teachers at Public Schools 59, 63, 158, and 277, in New York City; teachers in Bexley, OH; Philadelphia, PA; and Chappaqua, NY; teachers enrolled in TCRWP summer institutes; and teachers in my specialty courses and leadership groups. All that time you thought I was teaching you, I was learning from you!

Thanks to Trixie Della Rosa and Polly Luckett for your endless support and wise counsel. Everyone needs people in their professional lives whom they trust completely and can rely on. I'm lucky to have you both.

Thank you to the team at Heinemann who have helped make this book possible. Thanks to Kate Montgomery for seeing promise in the initial proposal (and giving it a critical read at the very end, *years later*) and for matching me with the wonderful Zoë Ryder White. Zoë, you have been one of this book's greatest cheerleaders. I am grateful for your critical questions, invaluable feedback, and enthusiasm. Thanks also to Patty Adams and Victoria Merecki, in production, and Eric Chalek, in marketing, for your creativity, time, and dedication.

Thank you to the team who helped make this book beautiful. Thanks to Joyce Boley, Danielle Dininno, Karyn Grant, Jessica Figueroa, and Kristin Bubnis, at Bowne-Munro

Elementary School, for hosting us for two days and spending so much time sprucing up your classrooms before you packed it all up at the end of the year. Thanks to Nick Christoff and Michelle Baker for taking the photographs and to Suzanne Heiser for your beautiful cover design and for making the interior of the book easy to read and navigate.

I owe much to Joana and her generous family, who have graciously lent the work that appears throughout the book and have stayed in touch with me through the years.

And finally, thank you to my family. Lola and Vivie, one of my greatest hopes for you is that you find a career you love as much as I love mine. Still, it's never easy to turn from you to the computer or leave the house at the crack of dawn to make my way to a school or airport or conference. Thank you for understanding.

Introduction

Like many people studying to be a teacher, I spent a lot of time in my college methods classes crafting beautiful and elaborate units of study. I can remember the process for one unit I created for my fifth-grade student teaching experience. I read through stacks of texts on the formation of the U.S. government and how a bill becomes a law. I planned field trips to the New York state capital, gathered up *Schoolhouse Rock!* videos, and collected numerous texts that I would read aloud and that my students would read independently. I planned mock trials and debates that my students would engage in and created quizzes and tests to evaluate student understanding along the way. I wrote out carefully scripted lesson plans that earned accolades from both my supervisor from the university and my cooperating teacher.

Looking back on that experience, my students did have a lot of fun with that unit—and a bunch of them learned a lot. But if I knew then what I know now, I'd have sent myself back to the drawing board.

All of that curriculum planning was completely devoid of the students in front of me.

I'd like to say this was a mistake I made only in my role as student teacher, but I actually repeated it time and again through my first years as a classroom teacher. Whether teaching social studies, science, reading, writing, or math—I didn't quite understand as I now do the differences between teaching a class of children and teaching curriculum or standards.

Some years, I reluctantly admit, I had groups of students who made very little progress. I could never quite put my finger on why this was. I didn't understand the difference between assessing students to check up on understandings and assessing students to form my teaching plan.

These experiences are the main inspiration for this book. I wanted to write a book to help you to really *see* your students so that all of your planning for students as individuals, groups, and a whole class is based in what kids already know, understand, and are able to do. I wanted to help ensure that the teaching we choose to do aims high enough and helps move kids to the next step.

This book isn't going to necessarily help you plan the specifics of your next unit of study on fantasy book clubs or writing realistic fiction. What it will do, though, is help you understand your students with a kind of depth that will allow you to tweak the reading and writing units you plan to teach to ensure you're meeting the needs of your students and to ensure you're giving each of them opportunities for success.

This book is about being empowered by data and assessment, not bogged down by it. It's about getting to know each and every student in your classroom well and feeling confident in your decision making because of your reliance on assessments. It's about reclaiming and reinvigorating the term *classroom-based assessment* for the current era, when it's all the more critical that teachers know how to analyze the work students do each day, in groups and individually. Because if teachers don't have their fingers on the pulse of students' response to instruction, who does?

If you are reading both this book and *The Literacy Teacher's Playbook, Grades K–2* (Serravallo 2014), you're going to notice some similarities and some differences. The overarching structure of the books is the same, because on a macro level what I'm hoping you'll take away from this book is an understanding of a process you can employ to study student work, establish goals, and begin consistent goal-directed instruction across grade levels. Much of the content, however, is different. Since so much of your success with the process described in this book depends upon how much you know about the teaching of reading and writing, I've included lots of specific information about what types of student work to collect, what to look for in that student work, and what types of goals are age-appropriate. Of course, K–2 and 3–6 are still wide spans, and a 200-page book can't explore everything there is to know about reading and writing at every stage, but throughout both books you'll find that I will direct you to resources and materials that will further support your grade-level-specific knowledge.

The four chapters in this book illuminate a four-step protocol or procedure you may use. Within these four chapters, you'll learn how to collect data that are helpful, analyze the data correctly, and make plans based on that data. You'll learn how to lead conversations with individual students to establish goals that will focus your work together, and their work independently, during your literacy time. You'll learn ways to manage these individual goals to help your reading and writing class hum with a productivity and intention that will have big payoffs for students. The four steps are:

- Step 1: Collect data.
- Step 2: Analyze data.
- Step 3: Interpret data and establish a goal.
- Step 4: Create an action plan.

These four steps will function like a playbook: the indispensable guide a football coach relies on to know just what to do in certain situations.

Chapter 1 details step 1, collecting data. Football coaches prepare for Sunday afternoon's game by collecting films of the opposing team's past games. They send out scouts to watch the other team play against different types of teams, in different types of weather, at different times of day. As teachers, we need to collect information from a variety of situations—both reading and writing—that highlight different aspects of a student. We'll look at five lenses for reading (engagement, fluency, print work, comprehension, and conversation) as well as qualities of good writing, writing process, and writing engagement. I offer suggestions on what the data might look like that will give you insight about each of these lenses, a rationale for why you'd want to collect the data, and quick instructions on how to collect it.

This book is about being empowered by data and assessment, not bogged down by it.

Chapter 2 gives information on step 2, analyzing data. Once coaches have all their data—their films and notes from the assistant scouts—they sit down and analyze it. Looking at which players are strongest in which situations and what plays the team tends to have the most success with helps the coaches get ready to make a plan. Of course, when looking at these data, football coaches have a great deal of content knowledge about what it takes to be successful. In Chapter 2, I offer you, the literacy teacher, the content you need to look closely at each piece of data and analyze it. Through the analysis, I guide you in noticing individual student strengths as well as opportunities for next steps.

In Chapter 3, we'll explore step 3, interpreting data and crafting a goal. From their analysis of the opposing team and their individual players' tendencies, coaches make generalizations about the types of plays that will have the biggest payoff in the upcoming game. They establish goals for how to deal with each situation. As literacy teachers, we'll go about the work of looking for patterns and trends across the data we've analyzed to come up with some interpretations, or theories, about what's going on with the student and what goals might have the biggest payoff.

The fourth and final chapter elaborates on step 4: developing an action plan. It's game time. Based on all the analysis and planning, coaches need to know what plays will help bring success to their team. For the students in your class, I show you how to take the established goal and make a plan, both short and long term. We'll consider how to follow up with ongoing assessment and track progress over time.

I wrote this book as if I were planning a workshop. Its structure is rooted in the balanced literacy, "I do, we do, you do" framework. Throughout the book, you'll learn *from me* and then *with me*. I'll act like your coach, so you can be a coach for your students.

I do: I model my process by sharing what I'm thinking during each step and offering a lot of content support as well. I chose one "case study" child, a fourth grader named Joana, whom you'll get to know well across the course of the book through all of her work samples. You'll be able to study her work and read along as I voice over my analysis of her work. You'll read my conclusions about her in the tables provided throughout the chapters.

We do: I enclosed work samples from a second student, Alex. Here's your chance to try what I'm writing about with a little support from me. I include some of my own thoughts about Alex's work in Appendix A. You can study Alex's work alone or with a colleague—although I recommend the latter. Just as a head coach depends on the advice and thinking from his offensive and defensive coordinators, your insights about the student(s) you've chosen will be greatest with many minds on the task. Alex's work can be printed from www.heinemann.com/products/E04353.aspx (click on the Companion Resources tab), spread out on the table, and passed around if you're working with colleagues. You might use work from one of your own students during this phase instead of, or in addition to, using Alex's work.

If you follow along with these two students I've chosen—Joana and Alex—you'll notice they are very different. Joana is the type of student who seems to have it all down, the child you may leave alone because you can't figure out what you might do to challenge her further. Alex will seem quite different. He's the type of student whose immediate needs are more visible, a student that teachers often strive to understand better. He's a student that might be the type identified to be in need of Response to Intervention or intervention support. Both of these students are the types of children I get asked about most often: the kinds of students teachers feel they most want support in trying to understand better.

You do: My hope is that after you've seen the model (Joana) and had some guided practice (Alex), you'll be ready to try out the process independently with your own students.

Throughout Chapters 1 and 2 I've included references to some of those authors whose work in the teaching of reading and writing has influenced me most significantly. I include these references because I hope that as you work through the protocol to develop a goal for your chosen student(s), you also discover a professional learning goal for yourself—and seek out some of the sources I mention to begin your own self-study.

Finally, I hope that by going through this process you'll be all the more attuned to ways that real, authentic student work contains some of the most powerful information we have to make positive differences in our students' literacy.

Ready, set, hike!

Chapter 1

Collecting Data

ASSESSMENT LENSES AND TOOLS

Everywhere you turn these days, the term *data* stares you down. Teachers are asked to collect "data," report "data," track "data." Principals hold "data meetings" where whiteboards, "data walls," are covered with information about students. Schools are reviewed and evaluated based on their "data."

To me, data are not only the numbers and letters, but the actual stuff that a student produces: a student's everyday work. With this book, I hope to begin to shift your thinking about what *data* means and help you see that much of what you can pull out of your students' messy desks is actually data. Sticky notes that students write are data. Running records are data. Notebook entries are data. Student writing samples are data. Book logs are data. All of these are; that is, if you treat them as such. If you don't *use* them, they may start to feel like unnecessary paperwork for both you and your students.

This chapter is the first step in a four-part protocol to help you know your students and make purposeful evidence-based decisions for cross-curricular reading and writing instruction.

✗ • Step 1: Collect data.

- Step 2: Analyze data.
- Step 3: Interpret data and establish a goal.
- Step 4: Create an action plan.

In this chapter, you'll read about a handful of assessment lenses for reading and writing and the examples of types of student work that will help you see your students through those lenses. I'll show you some examples and I'll encourage you to start collecting from your own classroom, right away. If you don't have artifacts like the ones I recommend at the ready, you might begin thinking about some lessons you can do or some time you can set aside for students to do the work.

▢ Lenses and Tools for Assessing Reading and Writing

I recommend organizing reading assessments into five lenses that teachers might use to get to know readers. My purpose in organizing assessments into these five lenses is to help you to look through a lens that may be most familiar first and then to suggest assessment lenses that offer new ways of teaching reading that you may want to explore (Serravallo 2010).

The five lenses I recommend using when assessing readers are:

- reading engagement
- reading fluency
- print work/decoding
- reading comprehension
- conversation

In this book, I won't stop there. I've also chosen to include writing. Reading and writing connections are important in assessment and instruction. When you notice similar strengths and needs in reading and writing, it gives you a way to make the most of the goal you provide for your student by repeating that work across parts of the child's day. When you notice an imbalance, you can use the stronger of the two to bolster that area in need of strengthening.

The lenses we can use when assessing writers are:

- writing engagement
- qualities of good writing

Following, I describe each lens; under each, I offer options of tools to use to assess with that lens in mind. You'll also find assessment ideas, or tools. However, I want to emphasize from the get-go that you get the clearest sense of a student if you use all the lenses. Seeing a student in light of only one or two lenses is limiting to you and the student. It may cause you to make assumptions about a child that are untrue or to choose to focus on something less important.

For example, if you only have a running record for Sarah, a fifth-grade reader, you know that she read every word correctly, retold in sequence after reading a short two hundred–word passage, and answered some basic questions correctly. However, you're likely to miss out on opportunities to analyze deeper comprehension, something that is essential to helping upper elementary school–aged readers grow. I recommend that you try to collect *at least one* student artifact from each of the following lenses.

Assessing Reading Engagement

When we consider a student's level of engagement, we are in essence assessing whether the child reads for pleasure or reads merely for school. *Engagement* refers to a reader's motivation and desire to read and her ability to read for sustained amounts of time. It's no accident that I list this as the first lens. Research has proven time and again that in order for students to improve, they must read for long stretches of time, with just-right material, enjoying their texts (Allington 2011; Guthrie and Wigfield 1997; Calkins 2000; Serravallo 2010).

You and your students may already have a number of artifacts you can examine with an eye to assessing engagement. One of the most powerful is the **book log** (see Figure 1.1), wherein a student records time spent reading, texts read, and number of pages read.

Reading interest inventories (see Figure 1.2) are surveys that students can complete by writing their answers independently or by answering orally during a conference. Student answers can offer insights about attitudes toward reading and their interests in general (which may help you to find books for them that will be engaging). For example, I might ask, "What do you do after school?" or "What TV shows do you watch?" Especially for students who are more reluctant readers, but really for all students, these sorts of questions help me match them to engaging books that they might not be aware of. For example, if there is a student who loves baseball but tells me she hates reading, I might suggest a Jackie Robinson biography or a Matt Christopher book.

Some students may be "teacher pleasers" who try to intuit what it is you're looking for. These students may not answer the questionnaire honestly or may write answers that they think you want to hear. Asking questions in an open-ended fashion might help to ameliorate this problem. For example, instead of asking "What's your favorite book?" you might say "Are there any books you like?" The subtle difference between these two questions is a lack of assumption. Kids know that teachers want them to read, but sometimes finding out that reading hasn't been great for them so far can be an entry into an honest discussion about how to make this year different.

4th Grade Weekly Reading Log

Name: Nestor

Month of Reading Log: _____

Date	Place	Title of Book	Level	Time Started	Time Ended	Page Started	Page Ended	Total Pages
9/8/2010	School	Horrible Harry	L	10:30 am	11:00 am	1	22	21
9/27/10	school	Horrible Harry takes the cake	L	11:11		24	30	6
9/27/10	home	Horrible Harry takes the cake	L	3:50	4:20	30	45	15
9/28/10	school	Horrible Harry cracks the code	L	10:10	10:50	1	7	6
9/28/10	home	horrible harry cracks the code	L	7:18	7:48	11	25	14
9/29/10	school	horrible harry cracks the code	L	1:40	1:55	25	39	9
9/29/10	home	horrible harry cracks the code	L	5:00	5:30	39	46	8
9/30/10	school	horrible harry cracks the code	L			46	53	7
9/30/10	home	Horrible Harry cracks the code	L	6:53	7:33	53	60	7
10/1/10	school	Horrible Harry and the purple people	L	1:00	1:40	1	17	16
10/1/10	home	pokemon		6:10	7:10	1	50	49
10/2/10	home	Pokemon		5:50	6:50	50	300	259
10/3/10	home	Horrible Harry and christmas surprise	L	6:53	7:23	1	21	20

Figure 1.1 Students use book logs to record texts' titles, the time they spend reading, and the number of pages read. When keeping a book log, students record the title (and author) of the book that they are reading. They record the start page and start time before they begin reading, and then they record the end page and end time when they finish reading. For younger students, you may want to use a modified version of the log that has less information to complete. You may even just ask them to tally the number of times they've read a book. An example of this type of log can be found in *Teaching Reading in Small Groups* (2010). Not only are book logs useful as records of what types of books students have read, but you can also use them to look for revealing patterns about students' engagement. Where are students and what are they reading when they are reading the most pages, for the longest time? Where are they and what are they reading when they are reading just a few pages, or for a very short time? You may ask yourself these and other questions as you study your students' reading logs.

Even when squeezing every ounce of data from book logs and inventories as a teacher, I was left feeling still at an uncomfortable distance from knowing my students' engagement as readers. I developed another measure I call the **engagement inventory** as a kidwatching tool (see Figure 1.3) to quantitatively discover time on task and observable reading behaviors (Serravallo 2010).

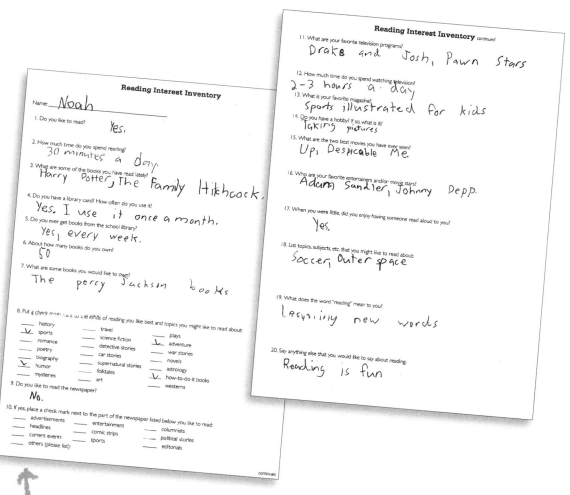

Figure 1.2 A reading interest inventory asks questions about a student's interests, habits, and attitudes around reading. There are many premade lists of questions that you can pull from by doing a quick Internet search, or you can make your own. You could also consider asking students to write you a letter about their interests and habits as readers, instead of answering a series of questions. For older students, you can give this inventory to the whole class at once and have them record their answers. For younger students, consider asking them some questions during a conference. Be careful that you ask questions in ways that are not leading but are instead open-ended.

Time/Environment: Names:	8:45–8:55	8:55–9:05	9:05–9:15	9:15–9:25	9:25–9:35		March 18
Mehak	✓	✓	✓	✓	✓		
Melissa	(T)	✓		✓	✓		
Jenny	✓	(NB)	(NB)	(NB)	✓		
Jose	✓	✓	(T)	✓	✓		
Ramon	✓	✓	✓	✓	✓		
Mark							
Desiree	(T)	(T)	✓	(○)	(T)		
Luke	✓	✓	(T)	✓			
Selma	✓	✓	(T)	✓			
Michael	✓	✓	✓	✓	✓		
Joana	✓	(NB)			(SB)(T)		
Erin	(T)	✓	(T)	✓	(NB)		
Maria	✓	✓			(NB)		
Verona	(Z)	✓	(NB)	✓	(NB)		
Rebecca	(Z)	✓	(NB)				
Charlie	✓			(NB)			
David	✓	(NB)	✓	(T)	(NB)		
Pete	(T)	(T)	✓	(T)			
Kenny							
Elizabeth	(Z)	(Z)	(Z)	✓	(Z)		
Margaret	✓	✓	✓				
Luca	✓	✓	✓	✓	✓		
Isabelle	✓	(Z)	✓	✓	✓		

Key:
✓ = engaged
W = looking at window
NB = writing in notebook
SB = switching books
Z = zoning out
T = looking @ teacher

Figure 1.3 An engagement inventory is essentially a system to record student behaviors as they read. To complete this, you'll kidwatch—spend time literally just watching your students—recording what you see for an entire independent reading period, instead of conferring or pulling small groups. Record anything you notice that might be an important key to understanding what kids do as they are reading—avoidance behaviors, distractibility, frequency of writing about reading, or signs of engaged reading. Feel free to create your own coding system for recording behaviors that makes sense to you.

ACTION → *Jot Down Your Ideas*

To borrow from renowned writing educator Carl Anderson (2000), I ask: "How's it going?" As you consider engagement and the three tools **(book logs, interest inventories, and the engagement inventories)** I've discussed, what resonates? What might you want to try first? Are there current students who come to mind you want to attend to first?

Write notes here:

_____

_____

_____

_____

To read more about engagement, see:

- Allington's (2011) *What Really Matters for Struggling Readers*

- Guthrie and Wigfield's (1997) *Reading Engagement*

- Miller's (2009) *The Book Whisperer*

- Smith and Wilhelm's (2006) *Going with the Flow*

Assessing Reading Fluency

Assessing a child's fluency is less straightforward than it might seem, because there is a chicken-and-egg relationship between fluency and comprehension. To read fluently, a reader needs to understand what she's reading. But to understand the text, a reader needs to be able to read it fluently.

Reading rate or speed is one piece of the fluency puzzle. You can quickly gauge a child's rate by asking him to read for one minute and recording how much of a page, or how many pages, he is able to read in that time. Keep in mind that when a child reads aloud, the rate is often slower than when reading silently. The recommendations for an appropriate rate in Chapter 2 relate to the reading a child does silently.

It's helpful to also consider accuracy, automaticity, expression (prosody), and parsing (phrasing) and take note of each aspect (Kuhn 2008).

- *Accuracy* refers to the reader's ability to identify words correctly.

- *Automaticity* relates to the reader's ability to recognize words right away, without having to apply any strategies to figure them out. A reader can have a perfect accuracy rate, but not be very automatic. This would sound belabored and choppy.

- *Parsing* refers to a reader's ability to accurately break up, or phrase, longer sentences into syntactically appropriate phrase units. Often, this means a reader needs to have some felt sense of how English syntax works, with phrases and clauses as parts of longer sentences. It may also mean that the reader is able to pay attention to medial punctuation like commas, semicolons, and dashes. If a reader reads without attention to correct phrases, comprehension could be altered. Consider Lynne Truss' (2006) clever picture books about grammar such as *Eats, Shoots & Leaves*. These books have the same phrase or sentence with and without a comma to teach children about the importance of these small marks on meaning.

- *Prosody* relates to a reader's ability to apply the appropriate amount of stress, emphasis, and intonation so that the reading sounds like how we talk. Without strong prosody, reading can sound monotone and dronelike.

A record of a child's oral reading can give helpful information about fluency. This can be obtained by taking a **fluency record** (Figure 1.4) or a running record (Figure 1.6), in the context of any oral reading during a conference, shared reading lesson, or partnership reading.

Justin and the Best Biscuits in the World by Mildred Pitts Walter

(HarperCollins 2010)

"So/it's about/time you got/home,"/ Evelyn/said./ She took charge/while their/mama worked/ each day./

Justin spread/his legs/as if/to take/a firm stand/ He hated/Evelyn/being the/boss/ He stared/ ahead/and said nothing./

"See/how he acts, Mama,"/ Evelyn said/ "He's that/way all the time/"

"Aw,/Evelyn,"/ Hadiya/said,/to protect/Justin./

He liked/Hadiya./ Everyone said/they looked alike:/ both dark,/ tall,/and thin/ Hadiya,/two years older/than Justin/ and three years younger/than/Evelyn,/was the/tallest/ At ten/years old,/ Justin was/already almost/as tall as/Evelyn.

Figure 1.4 Instead of listening only for miscues while a child reads aloud, listen with an ear toward fluency to take a fluency record. Make a slash mark each time you hear a student pause. Record information about the student's intonation or expression. This can be done as its own assessment or part of a running record (Figure 1.6). If done as part of a running record, you may ask a student to read one hundred words as you listen for miscues, then listen to the second one hundred words as you record information about fluency.

ACTION ⟶ _Jot Down Your Ideas_

As you consider fluency and the **fluency record,** what's on your mind? Do you feel this is an area that you want to look at with particular readers, right away? Do you already use assessments that allow you to look at your students' fluency? If so, are those helpful at looking at the same aspects of fluency as discussed in this chapter?

Write notes here:

_____

_____

_____

_____

To read more about fluency, see:

- Fountas and Pinnell's (2006) _Teaching for Comprehending and Fluency_

- Kuhn's (2008) _The Hows and Whys of Fluency Instruction_

- Rasinski's (2010) _The Fluent Reader_

Assessing Print Work/Decoding

When we look at a child's work through the lens of print work/decoding, we are training our attention to the work that students do when they come upon unfamiliar words in a text and what they do to figure out what those words say.

When children begin reading, many start by "reading" a story that they know well, turning the pages and telling the story as if they were attending to print. As you might suppose, this early reading behavior occurs primarily with familiar books that parents and teachers have read aloud to them.

After time in these emergent storybooks (Sulzby 1994) readers begin to be ready to use visual sources of information. Reading Recovery, Developmental Reading Assessment (DRA), and Irene Fountas and Gay Su Pinnell all have systems for leveling texts based on qualitative measures that help teachers introduce texts at a developmentally appropriate rate and within students' zones of proximal development.

At the most beginning levels, for example, Fountas and Pinnell (F&P) Text Level Gradient levels A and B, students begin understanding one-to-one matching and tracking the print with their finger and their eyes, left to right, following a pattern, and making sure their reading matches a picture. Beginning at level C, readers need to integrate the "graphophonic source of information," or information about letters and sounds, along with their knowledge of meaning and syntax.

Beginning readers check the picture to be sure they understand what's happening, and, still following a pattern, arrive at an unknown word. They use their knowledge of the alphabet and the sounds that letters make (letter-sound relationships) to begin to figure out what that word might be. As levels increase, so does the need to problem solve on the word level. Readers need to take on blends and digraphs, then later prefixes and suffixes, and then multisyllabic words.

Print work is best assessed and taught in the context of meaning, so that a reader is constantly practicing her ability to integrate what she knows about letters and sounds (visual), with what is happening in the story (meaning) and how language works (syntax). A record of oral reading, such as a **running record** (see Figure 1.6), gives a teacher great information about a reader's print work strategies in the context of real reading.

Analyzing an instructional-level running record is often much more revealing than an independent-level running record. Think about it, when the child reads with 98 percent accuracy, you might have only a couple of miscues to analyze. But when the child reads at 92 percent accuracy, there will be more miscues. When there are more miscues to analyze, patterns can be revealed that might otherwise be obscured. Therefore, when doing a running record, be sure to have the child read a text one level above that which he can read independently. Be sure to use a consistent coding system for recording a child's reading (see Figure 1.5).

Running-Record Note-Taking	
✓	word read correctly
Mother | (word read by student) Mom | (word in text)	word read incorrectly
M-m-mahh-mom Mom	sounding out behavior
Mother | SC Mom |	self-correction
-____ mom	deletion (student skips a word)
mom -	insertion
Mother | A Mom |	appeal for help
Mother |__ Mom |T	teacher told student word
Mother | R	student repeats

Figure 1.5 Shorthand Commonly Used for Running Records The table shows a coding system to use when taking running records that is recommended by Marie Clay (2000). Use this, or make your own, but try to keep it as consistent within your school as possible. When the coding of running records is consistent, all support teachers and classroom teachers from room to room will be able to use a common language to interpret a child's miscues and self-corrections.

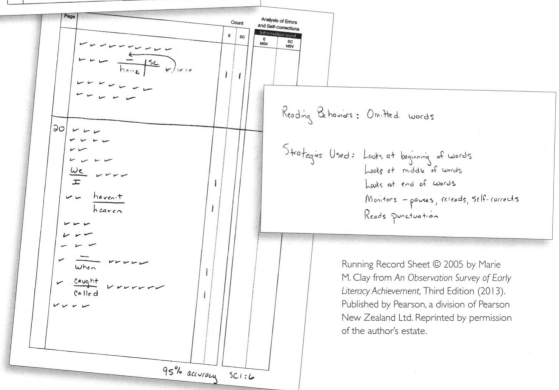

Figure 1.6 You can take a running record on a blank piece of paper or on a typed copy of what the student is reading. As the student reads, use a shorthand to record what you hear. For words read correctly, make a check mark. When a child says something different from what is on the page, mark it as such. This includes insertions, deletions, sounding out behavior, appeals for help, repetitions, and alternate pronunciations of the word. It takes time to become facile with taking running records. See Marie Clay's book *Running Records for Classroom Teachers* (2000) for more practice with the process. See Figure 1.5 for commonly used shorthand developed by Marie Clay (2000). See also the continuation of the running record—the comprehension component—within the next section, in Figure 1.10.

Running Record Sheet © 2005 by Marie M. Clay from *An Observation Survey of Early Literacy Achievement*, Third Edition (2013). Published by Pearson, a division of Pearson New Zealand Ltd. Reprinted by permission of the author's estate.

ACTION ➡ *Jot Down Your Ideas*

As you consider print work/decoding and the **running record** I've discussed, what resonates? Do you feel this is an area you've focused much on? What new ideas do you have about how decoding may or may not be an important part of reading instruction in your class?

Write notes here:

_____

_____

_____

_____

To read more about assessing and teaching print work strategies, see:

- Bear et al's (2011) *Words Their Way*

- Clay's (1991) *Becoming Literate*

- Fountas and Pinnell's (2008) *When Readers Struggle*

Assessing Reading Comprehension

Without comprehension, reading is just making sounds with your mouth. To truly read is to uncover meaning within a text, to understand what the author is saying, and to have your own reactions and responses to it.

Before children can even read conventionally, we can start teaching them the importance of comprehension. When she was two, I probably read upward of five books a day to my daughter. We snuggled into a rocking chair, gave the book our attention, and listened to the author's words. We stopped at places to talk about what was happening, we laughed when a character did silly stuff, and she occasionally reacted with an "I never knew that! Did you know that, Mama?" when we read something interesting. She knew maybe three letters of the alphabet (on a good day) at that time, but she understood that when you read a book, you strive to understand it.

Somehow, sometimes, something goes awry with students and they misunderstand what it means to read. Some children have gotten a message that saying the words right, reading at a certain speed, or making your reading sound good is all that matters. Consequently, comprehension falters. Or, other times there is something standing in the way of a child understanding a text such as limited prior knowledge about the topic or a memory issue that makes it challenging to carry information from one page to the next.

In an educational context, *comprehension* is often used as an umbrella term and includes a handful of skills and strategies that readers use in concert. Authors like Keene and Zimmermann (2007); Pearson, Roehler, Dole, and Duffy (1992); and Harvey and Goudvis (2007) have written about these aspects of comprehension and encourage teachers to make this the reading curriculum in grades K–8 (Pearson et al. 1992). The goal is not to assess for and teach children to be overly metacognitive when naming their process, although some level of metacognition does support comprehension. Instead, teachers should be aware of these areas of comprehension so that we can find ways to better support readers as they deepen their understandings of texts. These areas are:

- activating relevant prior knowledge before, during, and after reading a text
- determining the most important themes and ideas in a text
- creating visual and sensory images before, during, and after reading a text
- asking questions
- drawing inferences
- retelling and synthesizing
- utilizing a variety of fix-up strategies to repair comprehension when it breaks down

Keene and Zimmermann and others refer to these seven areas as *strategies*, though in my community at the Teachers College Reading and Writing Project, we call them *skills* (Afflerbach, Pearson, and Paris 2008; Serravallo 2010). Regardless of what they are called, what's important is that we have an eye on how well children understand a text. We can use these subcategories of comprehension to see the areas where children are strongest and those areas children need the most support in shoring up.

To determine what meaning children are making in a text is one of the trickiest parts of assessing reading, although it may be the most important. It's the understanding of texts that makes reading enjoyable. Also, in fact, it's the thrust of what's called for in the Reading Informational Texts and Reading Literature sections of the Common Core State Standards. Comprehension can, at times, be invisible. In our attempts to make reading comprehension visible—by having students write about, speak about, or answer questions about their reading—we are limited by the student's ability to represent her understanding using one of those formats. In other words, when students struggle to use the format, the depth of their comprehension may be obscured.

Figure 1.7 Taking a short story, or typed-up picture book, insert questions and prompts. As the student reads, he stops and jots responses and reactions to the questions and prompts. This assessment was developed by the Teachers College Reading and Writing Project. The site is often updated and assessments like this one can be found under Assessments at www.readingandwritingproject.com. Many teachers find tools such as this one to be helpful formative or summative assessments to assess the student's work within a unit of study.

For example, when we ask a child to retell a story aloud, and she has difficulty doing so, it could be that she didn't understand the story enough to retell it, or it could be that she has trouble verbally expressing herself. When we ask a student to stop and jot ideas about a character in a text and it appears as though his answers are very basic, is that an indication that he is thinking in a very simplistic way about his characters or that he has trouble expressing himself in writing?

The best we can do when assessing comprehension is to try to sample student understanding in a variety of ways. We may ask a student to **stop and jot** as he reads a short text or whole book independently (see Figures 1.7 and 1.8). We could listen in as a

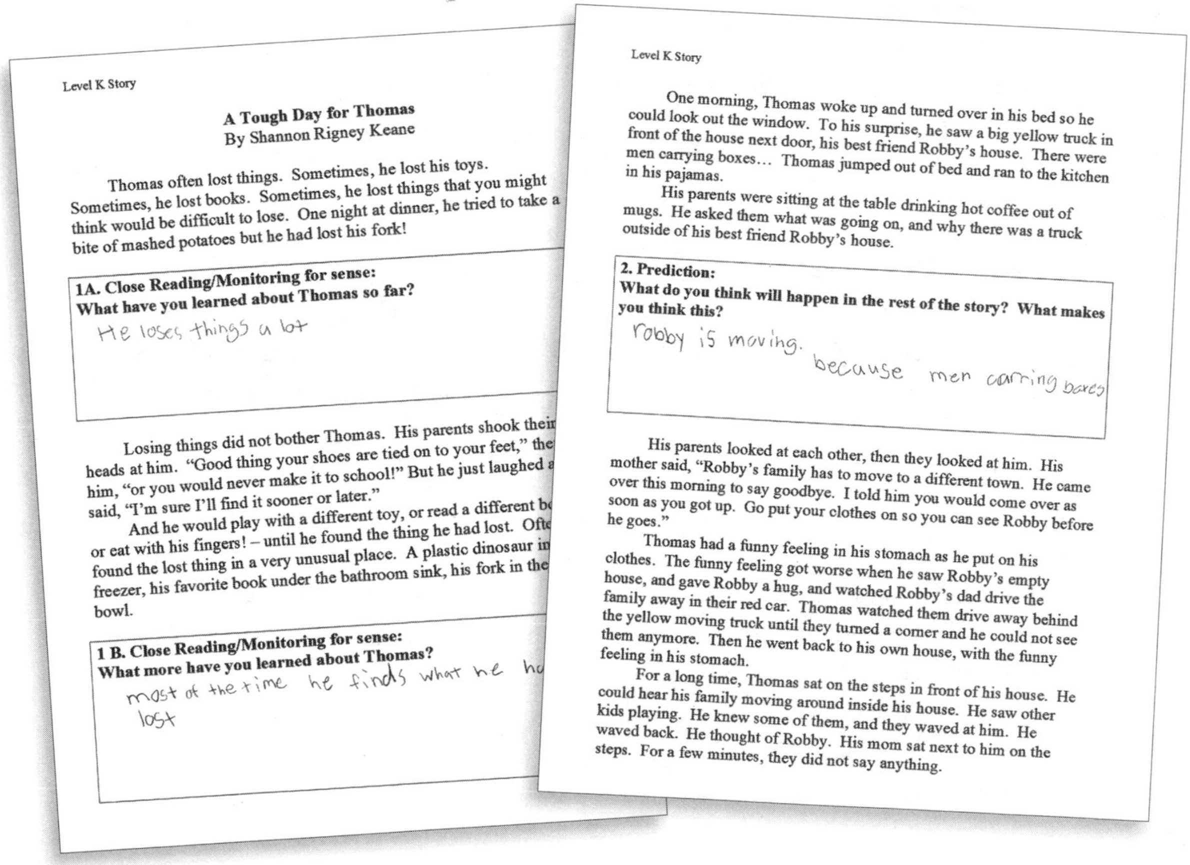

Level K Story

A Tough Day for Thomas
By Shannon Rigney Keane

Thomas often lost things. Sometimes, he lost his toys. Sometimes, he lost books. Sometimes, he lost things that you might think would be difficult to lose. One night at dinner, he tried to take a bite of mashed potatoes but he had lost his fork!

1A. Close Reading/Monitoring for sense:
What have you learned about Thomas so far?

He loses things a lot

Losing things did not bother Thomas. His parents shook their heads at him. "Good thing your shoes are tied on to your feet," the[y] him, "or you would never make it to school!" But he just laughed a said, "I'm sure I'll find it sooner or later."

And he would play with a different toy, or read a different b[ook] or eat with his fingers! – until he found the thing he had lost. Ofte[n] found the lost thing in a very unusual place. A plastic dinosaur in freezer, his favorite book under the bathroom sink, his fork in the bowl.

1 B. Close Reading/Monitoring for sense:
What more have you learned about Thomas?

most of the time he finds what he h[as] lost

Level K Story

One morning, Thomas woke up and turned over in his bed so he could look out the window. To his surprise, he saw a big yellow truck in front of the house next door, his best friend Robby's house. There were men carrying boxes... Thomas jumped out of bed and ran to the kitchen in his pajamas.

His parents were sitting at the table drinking hot coffee out of mugs. He asked them what was going on, and why there was a truck outside of his best friend Robby's house.

2. Prediction:
What do you think will happen in the rest of the story? What makes you think this?

robby is moving. because men carring boxes

His parents looked at each other, then they looked at him. His mother said, "Robby's family has to move to a different town. He came over this morning to say goodbye. I told him you would come over as soon as you got up. Go put your clothes on so you can see Robby before he goes."

Thomas had a funny feeling in his stomach as he put on his clothes. The funny feeling got worse when he saw Robby's empty house, and gave Robby a hug, and watched Robby's dad drive the family away in their red car. Thomas watched them drive away behind the yellow moving truck until they turned a corner and he could not see them anymore. Then he went back to his own house, with the funny feeling in his stomach.

For a long time, Thomas sat on the steps in front of his house. He could hear his family moving around inside his house. He saw other kids playing. He knew some of them, and they waved at him. He waved back. He thought of Robby. His mom sat next to him on the steps. For a few minutes, they did not say anything.

child discusses a book with a peer, and transcribe the **conversation** (see Figure 1.9). We might take a running record, asking the student to retell and answer some direct comprehension questions afterward (see Figure 1.10). We could read aloud to the child and ask him to **stop and jot** or **turn and talk** during the reading (see Figure 1.11).

Stuart Goes to School
by Sara Pennypacker

Student Response Form

Student's name ___Ashley___   Grade ___3rd___

Your teacher wants to learn more about you as a reader. Here are some directions to remember:

- Please complete this assessment on your own. Do not ask for help or use anything (dictionaries, websites, etc.) to help you.
- Each time you read, please fill in your reading log below.
- When you reach a page with a sticky note, read to the bottom of the page.
- Stop and answer the question on your response form. Include as much detail as you can from the book to support your answer. (It is fine to reread, but do not read ahead.)
- Put the sticky note back in the book.
- Keep reading!

READING LOG

Date	Start Time	End Time	Start Page	End Page	Total Time	Total Pages
10/13	10:00	10:20	1	15	20	15
10/14	10:00	10:35	1	41	35	26
10/15	2:00	2:25	42	56	25	15
				Total	80	56

Teacher: Please fill out

Independent Reading Assessment: Fiction © 2012 by Jennifer Serravallo • Scholastic Inc. 1

continues

Level K Story

3. Envisionment:
Picture what is happening right now. Describe it using as many details as you can.

he is sad that robby moved and that means he can not play every day.

Then, his mom said, "I know it's sad when someone we like goes away, but you have other friends."

Thomas said, "But I don't have any other Robby's. Robby has been my best friend for a long time."

"Yes," his mom said, "things that are important, like friends, take time. It will take time to make a new best friend. But you will."

Thomas thought about other things he had lost, and how he always found them sooner or later in unusual places, like the freezer, or under the bathroom sink, or in the dog's bowl. Losing a friend was different. He did not have another friend to play with that would be just the same.

4. Interpretation
What can you learn from Thomas' experience?

if you lose something you can always get it back\find a nother way.

Figure 1.8 A whole-book comprehension assessment, such as this from *Independent Reading Assessment: Fiction*, helps a teacher to collect information about students' understanding across an entire book. For narrative, students read entire chapter books and they answer questions about plot and setting, character, vocabulary and figurative language, and themes and ideas. For nonfiction, they answer questions about main idea, key details, vocabulary, and text features as they read. This assessment captures how well students can accumulate information and how well they are able to handle the text complexities of a given level (Serravallo 2012, 2013).

Stuart Goes to School
by Sara Pennypacker

1. PAGE 5 What kind of person is Stuart?

Stuart is a negative person becuase he thought it was going to be a bad day. Stuart Does not have any respect or manners.   E (P) A I

2. PAGE 13 What does "his ears begin to blow up" mean in this part?

Stuart was Embarrassed because he Never even knew that he was only in his underpants.   E (P) A I

3. PAGE 19 Why does Stuart work so hard to bring in something special for "Our Big Interesting World?"

Stuart wants to bring in something very Interesting to the class because he Wanted them to Forget what happen yesterday   E (P) A I

4. PAGE 21 What does Stuart mean when he says he has a "hole in his pocket"?

He has something in his pocket that can make a hole.

What does his family think he means?

His family think he has a real hole in his pocket.

Stuart Goes to School
by Sara Pennypacker

5. PAGE 32 Retell what's funny about this scene.

There was A No kids Allowed sign in the teachers room When they watch cartoons read comic Books and act silly.   E (P) A I

6. PAGE 36 Tell all the ways Stuart has used the hole from his pocket so far in the story.

To escape from the Boys Bathroom. To the hall to get Back to get back to the classroom.   E (P) A I

7. PAGE 40 How is Stuart feeling?

He felt sad

Why?

because, he thought he was a dangorse crimanle from making All the holes.   E (P) A I

Stuart Goes to School
by Sara Pennypacker

8. PAGE 42 What does Mrs. Spindles mean when she says, "Stop pulling my leg!"?

Mrs. Spindles means by stop pulling my leg is when Stuart came to class late and said "I had to cover all the holes and it means like stop playing around

9. PAGE 51 What problem(s) does Stuart's drawing cause?

The first problem was that the teacher Disapperd. The second problem was she was on the roof of the school. The third problem was that she could not get off the roof   E (P) A I

10. PAGE 56 What is something Stuart has learned by the end of the story?

Stuart learned that surprise is also a present.   E (P) A I

Stuart Goes to School
by Sara Pennypacker

Reflection

Was this book easy, just right, or too hard? just right or easy

How do you know? it was easy to read all the words

Did you like this book? no

Why or why not? it was too easy

Would you choose another book like this from the library? no

Why or why not? I like harder books.

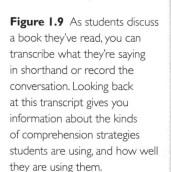

Figure 1.9 As students discuss a book they've read, you can transcribe what they're saying in shorthand or record the conversation. Looking back at this transcript gives you information about the kinds of comprehension strategies students are using, and how well they are using them.

Partnership Convo.   3/26   —Judy Moody

Marcus — She is so silly. she is always saying things in funny ways.

Elizabeth — Agree. she says one thing but means something else

M — Yeah like when she said "Make like a tree.. leaf alone?

E — Her brother annoys her

M — Agree. She doesn't play w/ other kids besides him though.

E — you think she wants to play w/ him?

M — No she's competing w/ him in band-aid contest

E — yeah. she wants to win. To beat him.

Retell:

These kids tried to trick their mother so they won't go to school. She tells them to stay in bed and then Dad came home. Dad was worried they had chicken pox.

Comp Qs:

1. (literal) Why does Dug put lipstick on his face?
   So it looks like chicken pox.
2. (literal) Where are the kids supposed to be?
   School.
3. (inferential) What do you think their mom will say?
   "You are in trouble. You should be in school."
4. (inferential) How do they feel about staying home?
   They like it and they think it's fun.

Figure 1.10 After taking an oral running record, standard practice is to ask the child to retell what she's read and then ask a small handful of follow-up comprehension questions, some literal and some inferential. Most commercially produced running records, such as the DRA or F&P's *Benchmark Assessment System,* include these questions. If you'll be taking a running record as a student reads a book from your classroom library, you'll need to create your own.

Figure 1.11 During a read-aloud, you may preplan a few places as stop-and-jot spots. After planning questions that assess particular reading skills, you can ask students to stop and record an answer on a sticky note, on a piece of paper, or in a notebook as in this example, instead of speaking their answer to a partner. For example, if you're trying to assess the students' abilities to visualize you might say, "Describe what you're picturing here." To assess inference, you might say, "What kind of person is the character?"

Stop-n-Jot   6-19

Book-Riding the Tiger by Eve Bunting

1. I am picturing a tall boy, who feels great and powerful because he is on the back of a tiger. The boy has an excited expression on his face.

2. I think Danny is really lonesome, and just wants to have friends, so he rides on the tigers back, only to get respect.

3. I think the tiger is not going to let Danny of his back to play basketball, only because the cop said "once you get on, it is very hard to get off."

4. I think the story is really about how you have to always make your own choices and not do what someone who is bigger and more powerful then you wants you to do. Also, you have to make your own decisions.

ACTION ⟶ Jot Down Your Ideas

As you consider comprehension and making student thinking visible through **whole-book assessments**, **short-passage assessments**, and **conversation**, what do you think you'll try first? What systems and structures are already in place in your classroom to help make your students' comprehension visible?

Write notes here:

_____

_____

_____

_____

To read more about comprehension, see:

- Harvey and Goudvis' (2007) *Strategies That Work*

- Keene and Zimmermann's (2007) *Mosaic of Thought*

- Keene et al's (2011) *Comprehension Going Forward*

- Keene's (2008) *To Understand*

- Serravallo's (2012, 2013) *Independent Reading Assessment*

- Zimmermann and Hutchins' (2003) *7 Keys to Comprehension*

Assessing Conversation

Student conversations about their reading—whether with a reading partner, a book club, or during a whole-class conversation—give teachers a window into students' understanding. As I've mentioned in the previous section on comprehension, we can transcribe these conversations and reflect on them through the lens of comprehension: what does the transcript reveal that a student understands or doesn't understand?

Conversation itself is also a skill. As the Speaking and Listening strand of the Common Core State Standards articulate, there are many aspects to engaging in thoughtful conversation (www.corestandards.org). Some highlights from the fourth-grade standards, for example, are:

- Follow agreed upon rules of discussion.
- Paraphrase information.
- Identify reasons and evidence a speaker provides.
- Report on a topic, tell a story, or recount an experience in an organized manner with appropriate facts and relevant descriptive details to support main ideas or themes.
- Speak clearly at an understandable pace.
- Use formal English when appropriate to task and situation.

Figure 1.12 As students speak about a read-aloud as a whole class, I try to hang back and take notes on what students are doing. I record who speaks and who stays silent (see the checks around a circle on the left). The circle represents the seating position of each student. Every time a child speaks during the conversation, the teacher makes a check mark next to his or her initials (or name or spot on the circle) and writes a brief transcription of what was said. I record what's said, and I record how I intervene to provide instructional support (see the transcript on the right). I can then return to this transcript and read through the lens of noticing what they are doing as conversationalists, and with the aim of setting goals for my class' work during talk time.

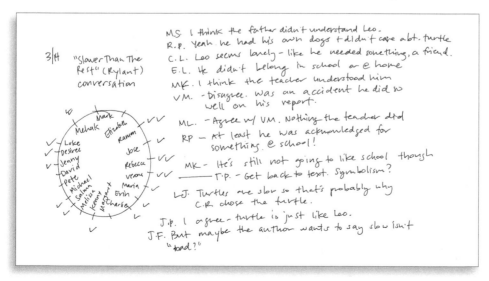

It is essential, then, that we provide opportunities across the day for our students to engage in meaningful conversation: about topics of importance to the classroom community, about books read together as a class and independently with partners and clubs, about their writing, about math, and so on. As students speak and listen, it's just as important for us as teachers to listen and assess. I am in the habit of taking notes during **whole-class conversations** (see Figure 1.12), **one-on-one**, and **small-group conversations** (see Figure 1.9 in the previous section). I use these notes as assessments from which to craft goals and develop teaching and learning opportunities for students.

ACTION ➡ *Jot Down Your Ideas*

As you consider conversation, reflect for a moment about the time your students have to talk in class and whether you tend to use those talk opportunities as also assessment opportunities. What will you try from this section?

Write notes here:

_____

_____

_____

_____

To read more about conversation, see:

- Bomer and Bomer's (2001) *For a Better World*

- Calkins et al.'s (2010) *Units of Study for Teaching Reading, Grades 3–5*

- Daniels' (2002) *Literature Circles*

- Johnston's (2004) *Choice Words*

- Nichols' (2006) *Comprehension Through Conversation*

Assessing Writing Engagement

Just as we considered reading engagement as an important factor before launching into the quality of a students' reading work, so too should we consider writing engagement. A child's attitudes and beliefs about writing as well as her desire to write are the stepping-stones to producing good writing.

We can also look at students' habits and process and consider:

- volume of writing (how much a student produces in a given time)
- motivation to write
- whether a student understands, and uses, a writing process

I recommend kidwatching and completing an **engagement inventory** (see Figure 1.3) for writing workshop just like you would in reading workshop. Having students keep a writer's notebook and **examining writing volume** over time is a way to study whether volume of writing is stagnant or improving over time. Also, encouraging students to hold on to all the parts of their process—entries in the notebook, drafts, evidence of revision on the draft or with add-on pieces such as sticky notes—as well as a published piece will give a bigger picture of what they understand about writing process and will also send the message that process as well as product is valued in your classroom.

> **For more information on assessing and teaching for writer engagement, see:**
>
> - Cruz's (2008) *A Quick Guide to Reaching Struggling Writers, K–5*
>
> - Fletcher's (2006) *Boy Writers*
>
> - Lehman's (2011) *A Quick Guide to Reviving Disengaged Writers, 5–8*

Assessing Qualities of Good Writing

When I was a new classroom teacher I spent three hours once a week studying student writing with Carl Anderson while he was in the midst of writing the book *Assessing Writers* (Anderson 2005). Carl put up a piece of writing and we had to say at least ten things the student was doing well. This was harder to do for some pieces than for others!

Then, we shifted our thinking and tried to name out every possibility for growth for that student. Then we did it again. And again. This experience of repeated practice, under the tutelage of a master teacher, equipped me with a framework I use every time I approach a piece of student writing.

Whether I'm looking at a piece of **narrative** (personal narrative, memoir, fiction), **informational** (all-about book, content essay), or **opinion** (persuasive essay, review, speech) piece, I apply what are commonly known as the qualities of good writing:

- meaning
- structure/organization
- elaboration/detail
- conventions

Ideas for ways to support the student jump off the page. I believe the qualities of good writing have a hierarchy of importance (listed in the order above) that I keep in mind when assessing writers and making a teaching decision.

In a way, assessing writing can feel a bit more accessible than assessing reading because we have a visual artifact that we can pack in our bags and take home and something right on the child's desktop to look at when we confer. Still, consciously choosing lenses for assessing writing is essential to be able to determine importance and to know what to teach first. Also, we need to provide varied opportunities for students to write and look at those different types of writing alongside one another.

Some writing we are assessing may have been through an entire writing cycle (see Figure 1.13). If working within a writing workshop, students receive a daily minilesson as well as one-on-one and small-group support with their writing. The final product should be fairly polished as it represents work over a good amount of time and guided practice from a teacher.

On-demand writing is writing that is completed in one to three sittings and asks students to go through the entire process of planning, drafting, revising, and editing independently. Without minilessons or conferring,

Figure 1.13 These sample pages represent the process one fourth grader took from the writing notebook to the final version of the piece. This process, in addition to the qualities of good writing demonstrated in the final version, will be important to examine.

5 partner prompts

11/1

This is important because animals have the right to live.

In addition animals are not made for clothes.

I used to think It wasn't a big Deal,

But now I think It is important to save the animals.
that it's not okay
This makes me realize to kill animals.

The suprising thing about this is that we should try to save animals and not make their species rarer.

Gathering Ideas

New and improved claim: It's not okay to kill animals.

Choosing a Claim

Three completely good, different reasons.

•1 Animals are diying because of other animals getting extinct, and It so happens that other animals are fed with that animals.

•2 Animals have their right to live and it's not okay for humans to hunt them.

3° Some animals help and save our trees, flowers, soil and grass.

Developing a Claim

this shows us the writing that students can do independently. It also is an interesting assessment of what students understand about process. You may want to offer an open-ended prompt to get kids started:

- **Narrative:** Think of a moment that is particularly important to you. Tell the story of this moment using purposeful detail.
- **Opinion:** Think of something you have strong feelings about. Write a piece persuading someone about your viewpoint.
- **Informational:** Think about something you feel you know a lot about. Write a piece teaching someone else what you know about that topic.

For both through-the-process and on-demand writing, keep an eye on your curriculum and make sure you're teaching a balance of informational, narrative, and opinion writing. The writing samples you collect for the purpose of this protocol will depend on where you are in your current curriculum. It's important that the student work is current, and therefore it's unlikely that the student will have current work from all three domains of writing.

Joana

Do Not Kill Animals!

Do you agree that killing animals just for sport or fur is wright or wrong? Well, I think it's wrong! I thing it's wrong becnuse they have their right to live just like us. When I read about what people were doing to animals. I almost wanted to rip the page out of the book! I don't like how people are treating animals. I think that it is not okay to kill animals and there are a lot of reasons why!

One reason for why humans should not kill animals is because animals have their right to live and it's not okay to kill them for fur and sport. For instance once I've read in a magazine that "if you kill an animal it seems as if you have killed a person". One time I had this expirience: The sun was shining and I was relaxing in my sleeping bag smelling the fresh air of the woods. Then far away I thought I heard a gunshot! "Did you hear that?" I asked. "What?" my father asked in confusion. "You must be hearing things because I didn't hear anything!" he replyed in suprise. "Oh, okay but anyway could I go for a walk in the woods?" I asked. "Sure go ahead" he shouted as I disapeared in the woods.

The fence was far away but I didn't care. Finally I came to a wired fence. And there lay a small bird. I thought that an animal killed it but I wasn't sure. Anyway I couldn't bring it back to life! That day I learned that even animals are like us and they have their right to live.

Another reason for why it's not okay to kill animals is because some animals are helping to our enviorment and our world. This show that not only people help the world but even animals. Some animals are ahelpful to our plants like squrriels. Some animals are helpful for support systems like cats, dogs, birds, hamsers and other animals too. Some animals are helpful for not letting too many animals eat too much of anything. Like foxes eat rabbits and if there wasn't any foxes the number of rabbits would grow and there would be less plants. In addition once I was quietly reading an encyclopedea in the section of animals and insects. Then my eye caught an intresting fact about worms. It turned out that worms actually helped make a better soil for plants! "Mom did you know that worms made a better soil for plants?" I shouted. She replyed, "It is intresting that some animals are helping in a way." Then I ran ~~away~~ in my

Final Essay

continues

backyard and just in time I saw a worm dive into the ground! That day I will never forget that worm because I knew that some kids were hateful to worms and I felt bad. Some times it accures to me that some animals are being helpful in a way.

A third reason for why it's not okay to kill animals is because people are killing animals food so that makes them endangered. In other words some animals are dying because of hunters hunting their food. Do you agree that some animals are dying because of hunters hunting their food? Well, I do. In addition I think we should try to not kill animals food. Also I think making their species rarer isn't right. For example one day the teacher anounced: "Soon, we are going to put on an animal fair. So I suggest you start researching as soon as you get home." Some students cheered and some students groaned. I was one of the cheering students. Each of us had to choose a topic about animals. I chose a topic about animals getting killed because people were killing their food. As soon as I got home I started researching. As the day of the animal fair aproching I was almost finished. Then finally the parents

came. By then my board was all finished. When my parent came to my board they smiled and said "Great job". I hugged them. That day I learned that even animals are important and it's not okay to kill their food.

I feel that people should be more careful with animals and try to protect them. It is important because animals have their right to live, they can help our world and us, and animals are dying because of people killing their food. So next time you see or even heard about animals getting killed just for fun as fur, think about these reasons and imagine if you were an animal how would you feel?

ACTION → Jot Down Your Ideas

As you consider qualities of good writing, what recent piece or pieces will you examine? Do you have any artifacts that could show process and/or engagement? How can you collect work that shows both **product** as well as **process**?

Write notes here:

_____

_____

_____

_____

To read more about the qualities of good writing, see:

- Anderson's (2005) *Assessing Writers*

- Calkins' and colleagues (2013) *Units of Study in Opinion, Information, and Narrative Writing*

- Culham's (2008) *6+1 Traits of Writing*

As you'll see in Chapter 3, student writing can help us to develop not only an understanding of the student as a writer, but also the student as a reader. Examining reading–writing connections gives us a more complete picture of a student. Crafting goals that are applicable to both reading and writing will help the student to have more depth to their work across the day and may ensure faster success with accomplishing a goal.

Wrap-Up

As you read through this chapter, reflect on the types of student work you tend to have at the ready. This may give you some insight into your own instructional priorities. Alternatively, it may reflect the types of work you felt your students needed the most practice with based on prior assessments.

Either way, I encourage you to set aside some planning and teaching time to make sure you've got a good sense of your students as both readers and writers. Make sure you understand your students in terms of their process and their products. Make sure you're looking to see not only what they do, but how engaged they are while they do it.

What's Next?

In Chapter 2 we take the student work you've collected and study it piece by piece to look for teaching opportunities. Make sure you've got a student's work to look at and/or print out the work of another student, Alex, which is available at www.heinemann.com /products/E04353.aspx (click on the Companion Resources tab).

ACTION →

- If you jotted down notes in each assessment lens section, skim them now and circle what strikes you as the most urgent action to take in your class or question to pursue. Perhaps think about a colleague you could team up with to collaborate on improving practices around assessing reading and/or writing.

- Collect artifacts to represent each assessment lens (ideally from the last couple of weeks) for at least one student. Keep in mind that some assessments relate to several lenses (for example, a running record can give you information about fluency, print work, and comprehension).

Chapter 2

Analyzing Data

MAKING DISCOVERIES FROM STUDENT WORK

> It is a fine thing to have ability, but the ability to discover things in others is the true test.
> —**Lou Holtz**

My almost-four-year-old daughter is a rock collector. Every mountain we hike, every friend's house we visit, she needs to bring a rock home. There's a pile on her bookshelf that I sometimes wish I could just toss one day while she's at preschool.

But I don't. I don't toss the pile because she *uses* those rocks. She holds one in her hand while she sits in my lap and I read her a story. She decorates her dollhouses with them, and uses them to build ramps for her toy cars to jump. One night I went to retuck her into bed and found one clutched in her hand.

All that data, that stuff you collect in your classroom—be honest, is there a pile? Is there a file drawer full of paper? Are there some days you wish you could just toss it? Don't! Just as my daughter's collection of rocks is useful to her, your piles and drawers full of "stuff" can be useful to you.

In this chapter, I show you how as we work through step 2 of the protocol, analyzing data. You'll learn how to look closely and carefully at students' work in order to make discoveries about them as learners. You'll see why you've been collecting all that stuff; you'll realize its *usefulness*.

- Step 1: Collect data.
X • **Step 2: Analyze data.**
- Step 3: Interpret data and establish a goal.
- Step 4: Create an action plan.

Are you sitting with a stack of student work at your side? I hope so! Reading this chapter will be a lot more useful if you have these samples at the ready. Decide if you'll practice using Alex's work (see Appendix A at the back of this book, or www.heinemann. com/products/E04353.aspx) or your own student's work.

Here are some essential reminders about the work described in Chapter 1:

- Collect samples of students' reading and writing work.
- Use current work, from the last few weeks, that represents about the same period in time. This is important because a student can show different strengths and needs if one were to look at artifacts that were collected many weeks apart.
- Be sure that you have samples that allow you to evaluate through each of the five lenses for reading (engagement, comprehension, print work, fluency, conversation) and writing work that shows process as well as product; one student work example to represent each lens is sufficient, and some work will help you understand students through more than one lens.

In the sections that follow, I provide practical help in analyzing each artifact to discover a student's strengths and potential areas for growth. I offer key questions to ask of the work, and some of the "look-fors," so that you can extrapolate what I'm doing with Joana's work. I summarize my findings in a table.

My hope is that you try the analysis alongside me, perhaps with Alex's work (available at www.heinemann.com/products/E04353.aspx or in Appendix A). If you are using Alex's work, I recommend printing it out or making photocopies so you can lay the work out in front of you and look across pages. You can also find my commentary on Alex in the back of the book in Appendix A—but no peeking until you give it a try!

After walking through my analysis of Joana, and trying the work on your own with Alex, you may try this process with your own students' work.

After supporting hundreds of teachers with this process, I have found that one of the biggest advantages a teacher has is a deep knowledge of content. While I do provide some support with the content you'll need, you may also use this chapter as a way to identify some gaps in your own content knowledge. When gaps occur, I encourage you to set a goal for your own learning and consult the resources I recommend in this chapter and in Chapter 1.

In this second step of the protocol, try to follow the advice of Peter Johnston (2004) and "notice and name" elements of your students' work. You may:

- Speak aloud, listing what you see. Be as precise as possible.
- Consider if what you see is evidence of a strength or a need.
- List observations in a chart, naming out strengths and potential areas for growth.

One important exercise is to make sure that the potential areas of growth we identify *are linked to the students' strengths*. That means we aren't looking for deficits in the absence of a noticeable strength. Instead, the teaching possibilities come from noticing something that is already a strength for the student. This ensures that our ideas for teaching goals are those that are within the student's zone of proximal development (Vygotsky 1978).

Keep in mind that what a student exhibits as a strength in November may be very different from her strengths in May. These strengths and needs change and develop across the year, and, consequently, the process of evaluating data and goal-setting based on that work is ongoing (see Figure 4.10 in Chapter 4).

If possible, work with colleagues as you analyze your students' work, because sometimes, looking at data from students we know well colors what we see. Trusted colleagues can bring invaluable insight and objectivity. Perhaps this could be work you do with a staff developer or literacy coach, or during a professional learning community meeting.

I recommend that you organize your conclusions and ideas into a simple table, such as the Table for Summarizing Analysis of Data (Figure 2.1) so that you may easily look across patterns and trends, which is what's coming in Chapter 3, step three.

Table for Summarizing Analysis of Data

Tool	Strengths	Possibilities for Growth
Reading log		
Writing about reading		
Running record		
Independent reading assessment		

Figure 2.1

One final quick word before we dive in: you're going to notice that you'll spend a long time on this part of the protocol. Don't panic! While it's true that the work of analyzing each piece of data individually is not quick, the process you experience here pays off in a number of ways—both for your students' learning as well as for your own. Also, keep in mind that I have collected many more student work examples from this sample student than you'll need for your own student(s). In addition, consider that this process is one that you'll want to use at first with one of those students who puzzle you most. Finally, know that like anything, with practice, the process of analysis will become more second-nature and you'll be able to move through it more quickly and easily.

ACTION ⟶

Decide if you'll work through this chapter with Alex's work (available at www.heinemann.com /products/E04353.aspx) or with the work of a student you've collected. Have it at your side. Also, make a copy of the "Table for Summarizing Analysis of Data" available in Appendix C, or quickly make your own table similar to Figure 2.1 in a word-processing document.

Using the Engagement Inventory

The engagement inventory gives you helpful information about the student's behaviors during independent reading. You can discover how well the student is able to settle into reading once the minilesson has ended, learn how long the student is able to sustain reading before losing attention, and begin to recognize the signs of engagement or distraction the student exhibits.

By using an engagement inventory, you can more accurately diagnose *if* a student has trouble with engagement, and *if so*, what sort of challenge(s) the student faces.

What to Look For

In the left-hand column are questions you can ask yourself when looking at the engagement inventory. In the middle column is advice on a precise place to look within the work sample that helps answer those questions. In the right-hand column is a list of ideal student behavior. Compare this ideal to what you're seeing in the engagement inventory, and use it to help you fill out the "strengths/possibilities for growth" chart:

Engagement Inventory Look-Fors

Question to Ask	Where to Look	The Ideal
Can the student settle into reading right away, or does she take some time to get settled?	Look to see if you have marked in the first box that the student is doing something other than reading.	The student can get settled immediately.
Is the student especially prone to distractions (i.e., noises outside the classroom, announcements, other students nearby) that interrupt reading for extended periods of time?	Look at places where you noted disengagement. Did anything happen at that time that might have caused it?	The student stays focused despite outside distractions. Or, the student is able to resettle after a brief distraction.
What signs of engagement might she exhibit?	Check the inventory for: laughing out loud, jotting occasionally to hold onto ideas, making facial expressions, and so on.	The student shows some signs of engaged, interested reading as indicated by some observable emotional response.
How long can the student maintain focused, engaged reading?	Count the number of minutes in a stretch of engaged reading.	The student is engaged for forty or more minutes.
What signs of disengagement does she exhibit?	Check the engagement inventory for writing on sticky notes more than reading, switching her book for a new one midchapter or midpage, staring out the window or watching the teacher, and so on.	The student does not show signs of disengagement. Or, when the student is disengaged, it is temporary and the student is able to quickly refocus.

A Sample Analysis: Joana

A look at the class as a whole shows that there are some students who struggled with engagement (see Figure 2.2). Six students (Melissa, Desiree, Erin, Rebecca, Pete, and Elizabeth) seemed to have a hard time getting settled at the start of reading. Other students seemed to have difficulty with reading stamina; they faded by the second or third

March 18

Time/Environment: Names:	8:45-8:55	8:55-9:05	9:05-9:15	9:15-9:25	9:25-9:35	
Mehak	✓	✓	✓	✓	✓	
Melissa	(T)	✓	✓	✓	✓	
Jenny	✓	(NB)	(NB)	(NB)	✓	
Jose	✓	✓	(T)	✓	✓	
Ramon	✓	✓	✓	✓	✓	
Mark	(T)	✓	✓	✓	✓	
Desiree	(T)	(T)	✓	(T)	(T)	
Luke	✓	✓	✓	✓	✓	
Selma	✓	✓	(T)	✓	✓	
Michael	✓	(NB)	✓	✓	✓	
Joana	✓	(NB)	✓	✓	(SB)	
Erin	(T)	✓	(T)	✓	(NB)	
Maria	✓	✓	✓	✓	(NB)	
Verona	(Z)	✓	(NB)	✓	✓	
Rebecca	✓	✓	(NB)	✓	✓	
Charlie	✓	✓	✓	(NB)	✓	
David	✓	(NB)	✓	✓	(NB)	
Pete	(T)	✓	✓	(T)	(T)	
Kenny	✓	✓	✓	✓	✓	
Elizabeth	(Z)	(Z)	(Z)	✓	(Z)	
Margaret	✓	✓	✓	✓	✓	
Luca	✓	✓	✓	✓	✓	
Isabelle	✓	(Z)	✓	✓	✓	

Key:
✓ = engaged
W = looking at window
NB = writing in notebook
SB = switching books
Z = zoning out
T = looking @ teacher

Figure 2.2 Joana's Engagement Inventory

ten-minute period (Jose, Selma, Erin, Isabelle). One student seemed to get very little reading done at all (Elizabeth).

Joana, a focused, quiet girl who moved to New York from Albania the year before these samples were collected, was clearly able to start the independent reading time engaged and stay engaged throughout the entire reading block—though she spoke and understood very little English when she arrived. The inventory reveals that she read solidly for the first ten minutes, took a moment to jot an idea in her notebook, sustained reading for the next twenty to thirty minutes, and then switched to a new book by the end of the period.

How I'd Summarize My Findings

Here is how I might summarize my conclusions about Joana based on the engagement inventory:

Tool	Strengths	Possibilities for Growth
Engagement inventory	• Has strategies to get started reading • Can sustain reading for long periods of time • Jots about her reading to hold onto ideas	• Is she switching to a new book in the midst of another chapter book? If so, perhaps working to sustain focus on one book the entire time.

Excerpt from main table on pages 97–101

Using the Book Log

Book logs give information about page-per-minute rate as well as book choice. But to fully mine their potential as an assessment tool, I encourage you to read between the lines, to suss out what these logs are communicating about a child's identity as a reader. Is he jumping into a reading life with both feet? What does the reading rate tell you about his appetite for reading? When you examine the child's book choices, what's your take? Avid reader or a bit of "autopilot" behavior going on? For example, I taught a fifth grader who plowed through just about every book in a popular series at a decent pace, but when I paused to consider it was March and she hadn't veered into other authors and genres, suddenly her reading engagement didn't seem as robust to me.

Looking closely helps you discover the types of books that seem to be appealing to the reader and which of these the reader has success with. By looking across the titles the student has read, you can discover if there is a particular author, series, or genre that he tends to gravitate toward. By comparing the titles with the reading rates, you can see if there are certain titles that seem to slow the reader down, perhaps indicating a lessened sense of engagement with the book. (Of course, it could also be the case that the student is simply slowing down to savor every word.)

You'll also get information about the reader's page-per-minute rate, total time spent reading, and reading habits at home versus at school. In general, readers of fictional chapter books should read at a rate of about three-quarters of a page per minute silently. Although it may seem strange that a child reading *Cam Jansen* should read at the same page-per-minute rate as someone reading *Maniac Magee*, the truth is that they *aren't* reading at the same rate. Word-per-minute rate should increase as readers read higher levels, and along with that increased word-per-minute rate, the density of print on a page becomes greater. In the end, it all works out to be about three-quarters page per minute. Reading rate is hard to estimate when reading informational texts since print size, layouts, and text features vary greatly within a level.

An interesting comparison can be to look at the child's reading rate at school versus at home. Or, when the student reads in the morning in school versus in the afternoon in school. For some readers, there may be a time of day or even a location that lends itself to more engaged reading.

What to Look For

It's helpful to have more than one week's worth of logs on hand so that you can look for trends over time. It may also be the case that the answers to these questions actually bring up more questions that you want to discuss with the student. For example, if you notice a good reading rate at home but not a great one in school, you might question whether the place the child sits is the best for him, or if there are particular distractions in school. Having this conversation with a student might give more definitive answers than just your examination of the log will.

Book Log Look-Fors

Question to Ask	Where to Look	The Ideal
What is the child's page-per-minute (PPM) rate in school? At home? In the afternoon? In the morning?	First, subtract the start and end times. Then, subtract the start and end pages. Divide the number of pages by the number of minutes.	Three-quarters PPM, or .75, regardless of time or location.
Are there certain books that the student seems to be more successful with (as evidenced by a good PPM rate)?	Compare the PPM rate of some types of books (genre, author, series) and others.	A consistent PPM rate is ideal, although a better rate with certain types of books can help you steer a student toward other books with which she's likely to be successful.

continues

Book Log Look-Fors (cont.)

Question to Ask	Where to Look	The Ideal
Are there certain books that this student seems to gravitate toward? Does the student vary authors, genres, and/or series?	Look in the title and author columns. Do you notice a pattern (i.e., similar genre or author or same series)?	There should be some balance in a child's reading "diet," although a child aware of her own tastes as a reader as evidenced by a clear pattern is helpful.
Does the student read books at an appropriate level?	If your log has one, look at the level column. Otherwise, jot the level of each title along the margin.	The student reads books she'll be successful with—at or slightly below her independent level.
Does the student finish a book before starting a new one?	Look at the last entry for a given book. Look to see if the last page number listed is the last page of the book.	Most students are better able to comprehend when they finish one book before starting another. There is a tendency to confuse details when multiple books are read simultaneously. Therefore, it's a sign of good reading habits to read and finish one book before starting another.

A Sample Analysis: Joana

Figure 2.3 shows examples of three logs that offer a one-month snapshot of Joana's reading habits. Early in the month, from May 3 to May 12, it seems as though Joana was only reading independently in school and not at home. At home, she was reading for *exactly* thirty or sixty minutes, likely the number of minutes that was assigned, but no more. It is interesting to note if children set a timer and only read the exact expected amount or if they read until they are done reading—which may mean the difference between a clock-watcher and a truly engaged reader.

I notice that she read a balance of nonfiction and fiction in the first few days of the month, but then dropped the nonfiction. She appears to mostly read on-level, reading level R and then moving to level S midmonth. Toward the end of the month she read a Barbara Park book (*The Kid in the Red Jacket*), which is below her assessed independent reading level, but frankly I think this is a great thing for kids to do once in a while. Keep in mind

Figure 2.3

Joana's Book Logs

Log 1

May Reading Log – Due Wednesday, June 1

Name: Joana Adult Signature: _(signature)_

Date	Home/School	Title	Author	Level	Start Page	End Page	Minutes Read
5/2/11	H (S)	Eleven					
5/2/11	(H) S	Eleven	Patricia R. Giff	R	1	4	2 min
5/2/11	(H) S	Eagles	same	NF/R	45	52	30 min
5/3/11	(H) S	Eleven	Tim Harris	NF	4	52	30 min
5/3	(H) S	Hawks	Patricia R. Giff	R	28	56	30 min
5/4	(H) S	Eleven	Tom Jackson / Harris	NF	4	52	30 min
5/4	(H) S	Cougars	Patricia R. Giff	R	57	82	30 min
5/5	(H) S	Eleven	Tom Jackson	NF	4	52	30 min
5/6	(H) S	same	Patricia R. Giff	R	83	120	60 min
5/7	(H) S	same		R	121	164	60 min
5/8	(H) S	Clarice Bean Spells Trouble	Lauren Child	R	5	62	60 min
5/9	(H) S	same	same	R	63	134	60 min
5/10	(H) S	same	same	R	135	187	60 min
5/11	(H) S	Danger on Panther Peak	Bill Wallace	R	1	49	60 min
5/11	(H) X	Danger on Panther Peak	same	R	50	96	60 min

Log 2

Date	Home/School	Title	Author	Level	Start Page	End Page	Minutes Read
5/11	H X	Danger on Panther Peak	Bill Wallace	R	97	168	60 min
5/12	H S	Zen and the art of faking	Jordan S.	R	1	49	60 min
5/13	H (S)	same	same	R	50	63	35 min
5/13	(H) S	same	same	R	64	103	60 min
5/14	(H) S	same	same	R	104	142	60 min
5/15	(H) S	same	same	R	143	189	60 min
5/16	H S	There's a boy in the girls bathroom	same	R	1	85	50 min
5/16	H S	same	Louis Sachar	R	189	200	10 min
5/17	H (S)	Zen and the art of faking it	Jordan S.	R	85	142	65 min
5/17	(H) S	There's a boy in the girls	Louis Sachar	R	143	195	40 min
5/17	(H) S	same	Jordan S.	R	201	226	20 min
5/18	H S	Zen and the art of faking it	same	R	226	257	20 min
5/18	H (S)	same	same	R	258	263	5 min
5/18	(H) S	The Lightning Thief	Rick Riordan	S	1	24	30 min
5/19	H (S)	same	Rick R.	S	25	56	60 min
5/19	(H) S	same	same	S	57	100	60 min
		same	same	S	101	150	60 min

Log 3

May Reading Log – Due Wednesday, June 1

Name: Joana Adult Signature: _(signature)_

Date	Home/School	Title	Author	Level	Start Page	End Page	Minutes Read
5/20	(H) S	same	same	S	151	276	60 min
5/21	(H) S	same	same	S	277	316	60 min
5/22	(H) S	same	same	S	317	375	60 min
5/23	(H) S	The sea of monsters	same	S	1	28	35 min
5/23	(H) S	same	same	S	29	75	60 min
5/24	(H) S	The kid in the red jacket	Barbara Park	O	1	50	45 min
5/24	(H) S	The sea of monsers	Rick Riordan	S	76	99	30 min
5/24	(H) S	same	same	S	100	155	60 min
5/25	H (S)	The kid in the Red Jacket	Barbara Park	O	51	64	15 min
5/25	(H) X	same	s	S			60 min
5/6	H S	The kid in the red Jacket	Barbara Parks	O	65	95	47 min
5/26	(H) S	The sea of monsters	Rick Riordan	S	156	275	60 min
5/27	(H) S	Confetti Girl	Diana Lopez	R,S,T,U	1	64	60 min
5/28	(H) S	Confetti Girl	same	R,S,T,U	65	112	60 min
5/29	(H) S	Confetti Girl	same	R,S,T,U	113	155	60 min
5/30	(H) S	Confetti Girl	same	R,S,T,U	156	194	60 min
5/31	H (S)	The kid in the Red Jacket	Barbara P.	O	96	113	15 min

Margin notes: social issue book; 5/31 Camp Confidential by Melissa Morgan S 35–96; 5/31 Camp Confidential by Melissa J. Morgan S 1–3, 45 min

that independent-level materials are those where students are still doing some work. For some, this work is with the print. For others, it's trying to improve fluency. Some students will be working on comprehension. To throw in reading that is considered easy once in a while has the potential to boost engagement and even free students up to do more complex thinking about texts.

One concern I have about her reading habits is that she seemed to bounce between books. She started a book, read eighty-five pages (see the second log where she started *There's a Boy in the Girl's Bathroom*), then read a different book, and then came back to the original book again. For some students, this could pose a problem to juggle multiple books at once. We'll have to look at some artifacts of her comprehension to see if this confusion is true for Joana. The one exception to this seems to be *The Lightning Thief*, which she read in five days (from May 18 to May 22). Knowing her curriculum at this time of year, I think that one of the books, perhaps the Park book, was a book she was reading as part of a book club, and the other book was one that she was reading independently.

Her reading rate seems to be fairly consistent and ranges from about three-quarters to one page per minute. There are a few exceptions here or there, but I wonder if this is a case of her reading rate being faster or slower or one of her not logging accurately (thinking back to the tendency for her to log *exact* round numbers of minutes each time makes me a bit suspicious). There doesn't seem to be a noticeable pattern in the difference between reading rate at home or school or for one author or genre versus another.

These examples show how you can develop several potential hypotheses about what a child is doing and why she might be doing it and not rush to label it one thing—sometimes what we notice leads us to collect or examine another kind of data, to get a full picture of the child.

How I'd Summarize My Findings

Here is how I might summarize my conclusions for Joana's book logs:

Tool	Strengths	Possibilities for Growth
Book log	• Chooses books that are a good fit, and in a variety of genres • Reads at an appropriate page-per-minute rate • Reads for about sixty minutes per day • Reads at home and at school • Reads an appropriate level	• She could learn to read until she's done reading, perhaps stopping at a place that's good for the book, not when the timer goes off. • She could focus on reading one book until completion before starting another.

Excerpt from main table on pages 97–101

Using the Reading Interest Inventory

The reading inventory gives you information about a student's self-awareness about reading habits, interests, and attitudes. As mentioned in Chapter 1, you can do this inventory orally for younger students or have older students complete it in writing.

As you look at a student's reading interest inventory, notice not only what the student says about reading but also what the student says about interests in general that may be applicable to reading. For example, favorite TV shows might help you make book recommendations based on topics or themes.

What to Look For

What you get from the inventory depends on what you've asked and how you've asked it. Open-ended questions are best because they often lead to more honest answers. You can also always ask a student follow-up questions, or ask him to elaborate, during a conference. Here are some predictable questions I ask myself when analyzing a reading interest inventory:

Reading Interest Inventory Look-Fors

Question to Ask	Where to Look	The Ideal
Does the student seem to have generally positive or negative feelings about reading?	Answers to questions such as "When was reading great for you?" and "When you think about your reading life, when do you feel sad, angry, or bored?"	I hope for honesty and an ability to self-reflect, less that a student has all warm and fuzzy memories. Knowing about a student's negative and positive experiences helps you create the best circumstances possible for him this year.
Is the student able to name a genre, author, or type of book that is a "good fit"?	Answers to questions such as, "What is your favorite author/series/genre?"	Again, I'd hope for the ability to self-reflect and that the student has some positive association with some type of author, series, or genre. It is also nice to see when a student has interests in more than one area.
How do the student's interests outside of reading match up with the child's interests in regard to reading?	Compare answers to questions about reading interests (topics, genres) to questions such as "What do you like to do in your free time?" or "What kind of TV shows/movies do you like?"	Ideally, there is overlap here. (When working with a student who is having trouble engaging, a mismatch here could signal that the student needs support with book choice.)

continues

Reading Interest Inventory Look-Fors (cont.)

Question to Ask	Where to Look	The Ideal
What reading habits and stamina do the child report?	Answers to questions such as "How much time to you spend reading each day?" and "How do you stay focused when reading?"	The child reads each day in school and every night, even when not assigned. The student should have strategies for staying focused and a reading "spot" that works for her.
Does the student seem to have an outside-of-school support network to encourage reading?	Answers to questions such as "Who reads with you at home?" or "With whom do you like to talk about the books you read?"	Ideally, the student finds some pleasure in interacting with others around texts—a family member or peer.

A Sample Analysis: Joana

Joana seems to have generally positive feelings about reading, writing, and school in general (see Figure 2.4). She is able to identify a genre that works for her (fantasy). I wonder if her interests outside of school—listening to funny stories—could be a way to introduce her to new books.

May Reflection

Dear Ms. Serravallo,

I love, love, love to read books, especially books in the fantasy genre. I also like to write and sketch. I love hanging out with my friends at the nearby park. They always have an interesting and/or hilarious story to tell me and we have a lot of fun together. I looked up to all of my teachers, and strive to learn everything I can from them. For the first few weeks of school, I was shy and never really volunteered to answer any questions or raised my hand. But, eventually, I began to feel more comfortable with sharing my ideas and I started participating in discussions. In fact, I think that my fourth-grade year has been my most outgoing yet.

Sincerely,
Joana

Figure 2.4 Joana Reflects on Her Reading Interests

How I'd Summarize My Findings

Tool	Strengths	Possibilities for Growth
Reading interest survey	• Reflects on her love of reading and in the fantasy genre specifically	• She could connect outside-of-reading interests to reading to help expand her book choices.

Excerpt from main table on pages 97–101

ACTION →

Take out the artifact(s) that help you understand your student's level of reading engagement. If you're trying out this protocol with Alex's work, you should be looking at his book log. After you do your own evaluation, you can see some of my thinking by turning to Appendix A.

Analyzing Writing About Reading: Short Text Thinking Record, Read-Aloud Stop-and-Jots, Reading Notebooks

In the 1980s, reading comprehension studies examined the thinking of proficient readers to determine what it is that they do when they read. They were able to distill comprehension down to seven aspects (Duffy et al. 1987; Paris, Cross, and Lipson 1984). These "comprehension thinking strategies" (Keene and Zimmermann 2007; Harvey and Goudvis 2007) first mentioned in Chapter 1 are:

- activating relevant prior knowledge before, during, and after reading a text
- determining the most important ideas and themes in a text
- creating visual and other sensory images before, during, and after reading a text
- asking questions
- drawing inferences
- retelling and synthesizing
- utilizing a variety of fix-up strategies to repair comprehension when it breaks down

Some have suggested that these seven aspects of comprehension should become the reading curriculum in grades K–8 (Pearson, Roehler, Dole, and Duffy 1992). To some curriculum developers, this means that students work inside of units of study where each unit explores one strategy in depth (Harvey and Goudvis 2007). Others have argued that students need to use these strategies in concert, when applicable, and instead suggest that units of study are best crafted around genres or purposes for reading, with multiple reading strategies being utilized within a unit (Calkins 2011).

Either way, since the popularization of reading workshop where students read self-selected independent-level texts, these seven skills have been an important foundation for reading instruction in America's schools.

Now, with the advent of the Common Core State Standards (CCSS), a level of deep comprehension is expected of all students. Look at the Reading Literature Standards and Reading Information Standards for a portrait of the types of understanding, analysis, comparison, and insight that are expected. While the following is by no means exhaustive, in fourth grade, these standards articulate some of what students are expected to do. While the standards may not use the same language as the seven skills listed earlier, they are essentially asking students to do the same things to get meaning from texts. For example:

- determine main idea and key details when summarizing an informational text (RI 4.2) is determining important ideas and retelling/synthesizing
- compare and contrast a firsthand and secondhand account of the same event or topic (RI 4.6) is synthesizing
- integrate information about two texts on the same topic (RI 4.9) is synthesizing
- use examples when drawing inferences (RL 4.1) is inferring and retelling
- interpret theme (RL 4.2) is determining important themes
- describe characters, settings, and events in depth (RL 4.3) is inferring, retelling, synthesizing, and determining importance

What to Look For

While the seven comprehension skills offer us a helpful framework for examining student's thinking, understanding if students are getting the most from their reading isn't as simple as a seven-item checklist. It's important, then, that you aren't looking simply at evidence for or absence of skills. Instead, it's important to consider how deep a student's work reaches within a particular skill.

You might, for example, ask students to respond to prompts you've prepared during a read-aloud. Since all students are responding to the same book at an identical spot, it will be easy for you to compare their answers. You can sort their responses to the same question in piles. Responses that seem basic go in one pile, those that feel on-target go in a second pile, and those that are especially sophisticated go in a third pile. These piles will give you a sense of how a child's work *within a strategy* could become deeper and deeper (Serravallo 2010).

For example, I recently asked a fourth-grade class to stop and jot what they pictured as I read a scene from the book *Those Shoes* by Maribeth Boelts. In the spot I stopped, the narrator tells about a boy, Jeremy, looking at shoes in a thrift store window. In the picture you seem him standing beside his grandmother, holding her hand. The setting looks like a city, with buildings close together. A pigeon and a bus stop are in the foreground.

Sample student responses can be seen in Figure 2.5. You might notice that in the most basic of the responses, the student simply named what was in the text and pictures. In the more sophisticated response, the child added in extra detail, inferring a bit about the character's feelings and describing Jeremy's facial expressions based on those emotions. In the most sophisticated response, the reader added in details about not only Jeremy but also the setting, using multisensory details, offering details beyond what the author describes.

Figure 2.5 Sample Student Responses from a Stop-and-Jot While Reading *Those Shoes* by Maribeth Boelts

J+G look longingly in window. Eyes wide. Bus brakes squeal, Smell of pizza from next door. J+G are focused only on shoes in window.

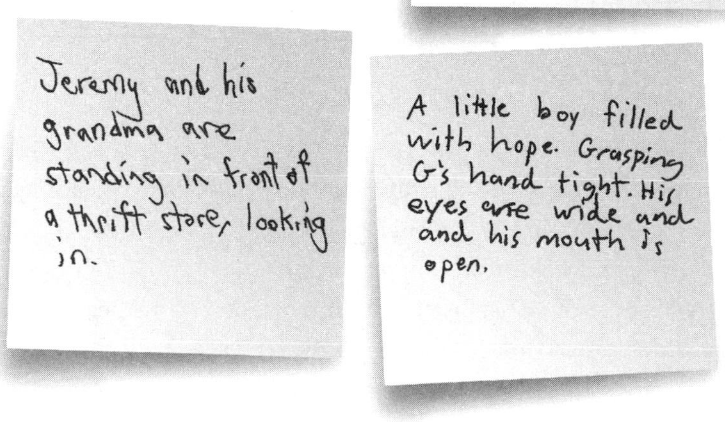

Jeremy and his grandma are standing in front of a thrift store, looking in.

A little boy filled with hope. Grasping G's hand tight. His eyes are wide and and his mouth is open.

While it is tempting for me to break down each and every reading skill into some theoretical learning progression, naming the qualities of basic to sophisticated thinking, the truth is that it's a bit more complicated than that. What would be considered a sophisticated response for a third grader is not the same thing as what would be considered a sophisticated response for a fifth grader. What would be considered a basic response for a child reading *Frog and Toad* is not the same as what would be considered a basic response for a child reading *Freak the Mighty*.

So, what's a teacher to do? There are a few options that will help you start to develop a frame of mind for thinking in this way. One is the CCSS. These standards can serve as a rough continuum that gives us a sense of what to expect, by year's end, at each grade level. Each numbered standard is described along a progression—so, for example, Standard 5.2 asks a fifth grader to do slightly more than what Standard 4.2 asks of a fourth grader.

Another option is to look at some other continuums that have been published by educational researchers that you trust. I've found Fountas and Pinnell's *The Continuum of Literacy Learning* (2010) to be incredibly helpful in understanding how texts get more complex

Comprehension Look-Fors

Question to Ask	Where to Look	The Ideal
What reading skills does the student tend to use?	Look across several days' worth of reading notebook entries or stop-and-jots on sticky notes.	The student uses a balance of skills when approaching a text. The student doesn't simply use a skill when it's mentioned in the day's minilesson, but instead the student knows when to use a skill to enhance his understanding of a text.
How deep is the work the student is doing?	Look at a couple of samples of work where the student uses the *same skill* (i.e., inferring).	Compare the student's work against a standard you trust for the given grade level and/or level of text complexity (e.g., Serravallo's *Independent Reading Assessment* [2012, 2013] or Fountas and Pinnell's *The Continuum of Literacy Learning* [2010], or the CCSS [2010]).

and what grade-level work looks like. Ellin Keene's *Assessing Comprehension Thinking Strategies* (2006) gives a rubric of sorts for evaluating student's writing about reading from short texts. Like a continuum, she names several "levels" for how to notice evidence of strategies on a more basic to most sophisticated level. See also my books *Independent Reading Assessment: Fiction* (2012), which helps teachers know what to expect of readers by reading level when reading literature, and *Independent Reading Assessment: Nonfiction* (2013), which does the same for informational texts (more on that in the next section).

You could also do as I did: with a group of colleagues, sit around a table and sort student writing about reading from your grade level. Be sure that you're comparing apples to apples: look at the students at the same grade level answering the same question from the same spot in the same book. From this, you can develop your own theoretical learning progressions.

A Sample Analysis: Joana

The two pages of writing about reading (Figure 2.6) come from Joana's reading note-book, which in her classroom is known as a "Book Lover's Book." Joana and other students in her class are given a long list of open-ended ways to respond to literature, and, as homework, are asked to write a response of no particular length to evidence what they are thinking about their reading.

In her entry on May 17, Joana muses about a lesson in the story. She states that one lesson she can take away from the text is that it's hard to fit in. She provides textual evidence from a couple of places in the story to show how Bradley has a hard time fitting in. In both this and her May 19 entry, she uses "social issues" as a way to help her make interpretations. She also empathizes with the character in analyzing those interpretations. In this example, she is doing the work called for in the Reading Literature Standards 2. She has identified a theme (or "lesson") in the story and supports her thinking with textual evidence. In discussing how the character reacts, she's actually doing the work described in Standard 2 *for fifth grade*. Using what I know about texts at this level, however, I know that stories often have more than one possible interpretation. I could deepen the work she's doing by encouraging her to discuss multiple possibilities for theme, encouraging her to think of the less obvious themes and ideas in the text.

She also mentions a secondary character, Carla, and the effect she has on Bradley: Carla helps him to change. This shows that she is on the lookout for ways that secondary characters can affect main characters and how characters are likely to change in a book. This is some of the work described in CCSS RL Standard 4.3. She could be encouraged do more work with secondary characters, describing in detail how they are also developed,

Figure 2.6 Excerpt from Joana's Reading Notebook

HW

5/17

Q.1. The text "There's A Boy in the Girl's Bathroom" is trying to teach me that sometimes you have to dig deep to find out what kind of person you want to be. This book talks about a boy named Bradley who is having trouble fitting in with others because of his behavior. But Carla, Bradley's counselor, helps him understand that being nasty to other people doesn't help him to make friends. I think the authors purpose for writing this book is to teach the reader about fitting in and how it's hard for some people to do that. One of those people is Bradley. First, Bradley has trouble fitting because he bullies other people. That made him disliked. But, with the help of Carla he became a better person. The author expressed the social issue of fitting in by writing the story of Bradley and how he had trouble fitting in. From reading this book I learned how bad people must feel when they try to fit in. I enjoyed reading this book. By reading it I

realized how not fitting in feels.

5/19

HW

Bradley overcomes his issue of fitting in by talking to Clara. Clara is a great help to Bradley because she helps him understand that being a bully just makes him more hated by the other kids. But also Bradley, uses his power of being disliked by the other students, to teach himself to ignore what other people say about himself. But, as time passed Bradley became more and more sensitive. Bradley's reaction to the social issue he faces is pretty bad. Instead of being nice and caring he is mean and non-selfish. Like for example he wants to beat up Melinda, Colleen and Lori just because they are saying hello to Jeff his best friend. Another strange thing is that he pays him to be his friend. But still thats how Bradley thinks you get friends. But in the end with Carla's help he becomes a better person.

perhaps also providing more textual evidence to support her thinking.

In her May 19 entry, she describes Bradley as "a bully" and, later, "sensitive." She writes that "instead of being nice and caring he is mean and selfish." One strength of hers is that she is able to use words to describe the character. I would stretch her abilities to infer about character by teaching her to use more *precise* language to describe the character and to also try to see the character with more complexity. Right now, she uses simplistic language and sees the character simply as being one way in the beginning and a different way in the end. This work again relates to CCSS RL 4.3.

All of Joana's writing in the entire notebook is about her fiction reading; there is nothing about her nonfiction reading. As you can tell from her log, she was reading nonfiction books at this time, yet seems to always choose to respond to her fiction reading in her Book Lover's Book. A goal for her would be to apply the same analysis she applies to fiction to her nonfiction reading.

How I'd Summarize My Findings

To summarize my conclusions from Joana's writing about reading, I'd write:

Tool	Strengths	Possibilities for Growth
Writing about reading	• Makes interpretations • Uses social issues as a way to make interpretations • Empathizes with characters • Uses words to describe characters • Provides some text evidence	• She could develop interpretations that are less obvious. • She could see characters in a more complex way. • She could analyze secondary characters. • She could use more precise language when analyzing characters. • She could apply the same level of analysis to nonfiction books. • She could provide more detailed text evidence.

Excerpt from main table on pages 97–101

📖 Analyzing a Whole-Book Comprehension Assessment

By the time readers get to chapter books, around the middle of second grade, running records begin to be less helpful in diagnosing instructional next steps. Longer chapter books offer an array of unique comprehension challenges. Students not only need to understand only the plot and characters and setting in the moment, but they also need to be able to accumulate and synthesize information across dozens and eventually hundreds of pages.

Likewise, teachers need to know what to expect of chapter book readers. When conferring with readers in longer books, especially those that are less familiar to the teacher, it's important to have a sense of the ways that leveled chapter books get more complex, and to look for **evidence** of students handling these challenges well. Plot and setting, character, vocabulary and figurative language, and themes and ideas all contribute to the complexity of fiction and are lenses through which teachers can assess students' reading proficiencies in fiction. In nonfiction texts, teachers examine students' ability to determine main idea, key details, the meaning of vocabulary, and information from text features to assess students' facility with nonfiction. (See Serravallo *Independent Reading Assessment for Fiction* 2012, Serravallo *Independent Reading Assessment for Nonfiction* 2013).

Whatever the tool you decide to use, I strongly encourage you to consider the value of understanding how your students are handling the complexities of the given level they are reading and to have an eye on how well students are accumulating and synthesizing longer swathes of text. See Figures 2.7 to 2.14 (from Serravallo 2012, 2013) for a summarized view of ways that expectations for readers increase as the text gets more complex.

Increasing Expectations for Comprehension in Literature

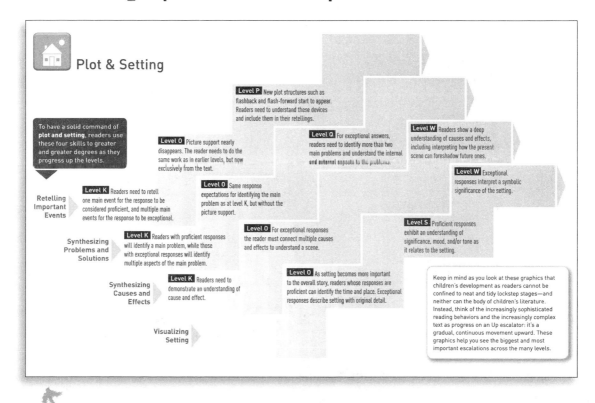

Figure 2.7
Increasing Expectations for Understanding Plot and Setting as Texts Become More Complex

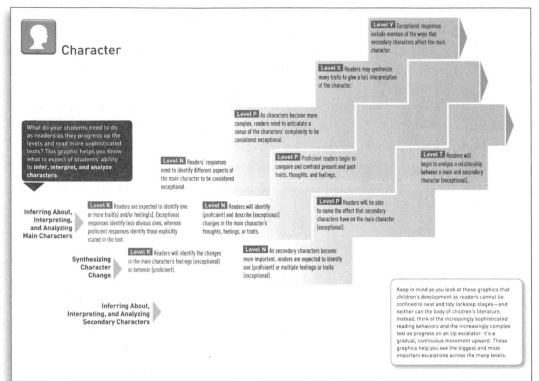

Character

What do your students need to do as readers as they progress up the levels and read more sophisticated texts? This graphic helps you know what to expect of students' ability to **infer, interpret, and analyze characters.**

Level V Exceptional responses include mention of the ways that secondary characters affect the main character.

Level S Readers may synthesize many traits to give a full interpretation of the character.

Level P As characters become more complex, readers need to articulate a sense of the characters' complexity to be considered exceptional.

Level N Readers' responses need to identify different aspects of the main character to be considered exceptional.

Level P Proficient readers begin to compare and contrast present and past traits, thoughts, and feelings.

Level T Readers will begin to analyze a relationship between a main and secondary character (exceptional).

Inferring About, Interpreting, and Analyzing Main Characters

Level K Readers are expected to identify one or more trait(s) and/or feeling(s). Exceptional responses identify less obvious ones, whereas proficient responses identify those explicitly stated in the text.

Level N Readers will identify (proficient) and describe (exceptional) changes in the main character's thoughts, feelings, or traits.

Level P Readers will be able to name the effect that secondary characters have on the main character (exceptional).

Synthesizing Character Change

Level K Readers will identify the changes in the main character's feelings (exceptional) or behavior (proficient).

Level N As secondary characters become more important, readers are expected to identify one (proficient) or multiple feelings or traits (exceptional).

Inferring About, Interpreting, and Analyzing Secondary Characters

Keep in mind as you look at these graphics that children's development as readers cannot be confined to neat and tidy lockstep stages—and neither can the body of children's literature. Instead, think of the increasingly sophisticated reading behaviors and the increasingly complex text as progress on an Up escalator: it's a gradual, continuous movement upward. These graphics help you see the biggest and most important escalations across the many levels.

Figure 2.8
Increasing Expectations for Understanding Character as Texts Become More Complex

---

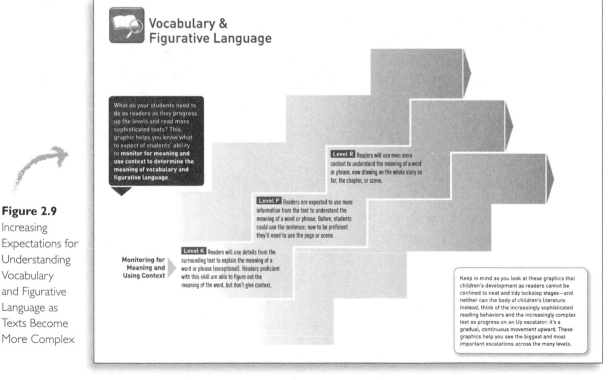

Vocabulary & Figurative Language

What do your students need to do as readers as they progress up the levels and read more sophisticated texts? This graphic helps you know what to expect of students' ability to **monitor for meaning and use context to determine the meaning of vocabulary and figurative language.**

Level R Readers will use even more context to understand the meaning of a word or phrase, now drawing on the whole story so far, the chapter, or scene.

Level P Readers are expected to use more information from the text to understand the meaning of a word or phrase. Before, students could use the sentence; now to be proficient they'll need to use the page or scene.

Monitoring for Meaning and Using Context

Level K Readers will use details from the surrounding text to explain the meaning of a word or phrase (exceptional). Readers proficient with this skill are able to figure out the meaning of the word, but don't give context.

Keep in mind as you look at these graphics that children's development as readers cannot be confined to neat and tidy lockstep stages—and neither can the body of children's literature. Instead, think of the increasingly sophisticated reading behaviors and the increasingly complex text as progress on an Up escalator: it's a gradual, continuous movement upward. These graphics help you see the biggest and most important escalations across the many levels.

Figure 2.9
Increasing Expectations for Understanding Vocabulary and Figurative Language as Texts Become More Complex

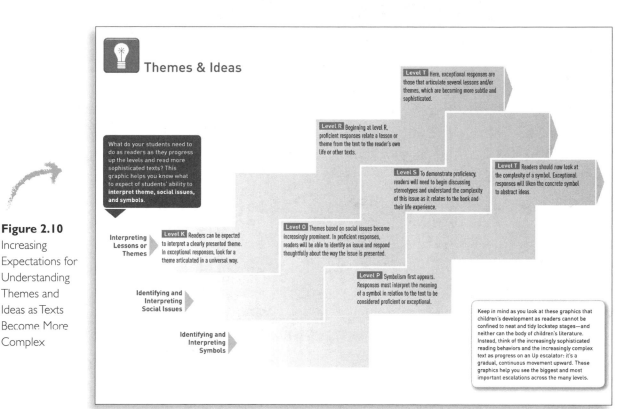

Figure 2.10
Increasing Expectations for Understanding Themes and Ideas as Texts Become More Complex

Increasing Expectations for Comprehension of Informational Texts

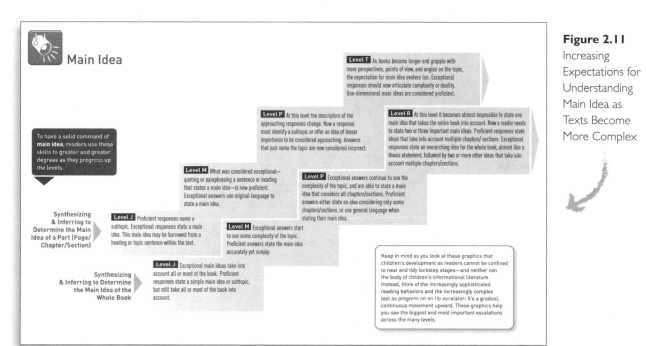

Figure 2.11
Increasing Expectations for Understanding Main Idea as Texts Become More Complex

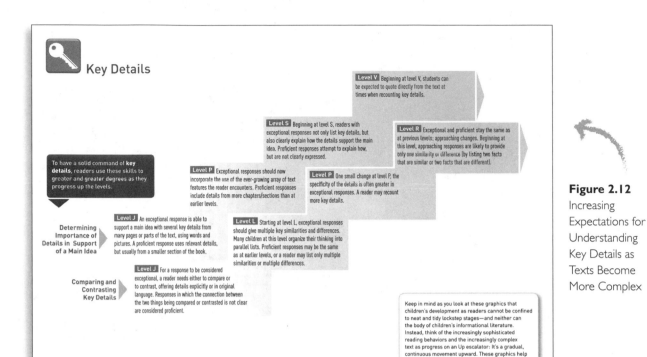

Key Details

To have a solid command of key details, readers use these skills to greater and greater degrees as they progress up the levels.

Determining Importance of Details in Support of a Main Idea

Level J An exceptional response is able to support a main idea with several key details from many pages or parts of the text, using words and pictures. A proficient response uses relevant details, but usually from a smaller section of the book.

Level L Starting at level L, exceptional responses should give multiple key similarities and differences. Many children at this level organize their thinking into parallel lists. Proficient responses may be the same as at earlier levels, or a reader may list only multiple similarities or multiple differences.

Level P Exceptional responses should now incorporate the use of the ever-growing array of text features the reader encounters. Proficient responses include details from more chapters/sections than at earlier levels.

Level P One small change at level P, the specificity of the details is often greater in exceptional responses. A reader may recount more key details.

Level S Beginning at level S, readers with exceptional responses not only list key details, but also clearly explain how the details support the main idea. Proficient responses attempt to explain how, but are not clearly expressed.

Level R Exceptional and proficient stay the same as at previous levels; approaching changes. Beginning at this level, approaching responses are likely to provide only one similarity or difference (by listing two facts that are similar or two facts that are different).

Level V Beginning at level V, students can be expected to quote directly from the text at times when recounting key details.

Comparing and Contrasting Key Details

Level J For a response to be considered exceptional, a reader needs either to compare or to contrast, offering details explicitly or in original language. Responses in which the connection between the two things being compared or contrasted is not clear are considered proficient.

Keep in mind as you look at these graphics that children's development as readers cannot be confined to neat and tidy lockstep stages—and neither can the body of children's informational literature. Instead, think of the increasingly sophisticated reading behaviors and the increasingly complex text as progress on an Up escalator: It's a gradual, continuous movement upward. These graphics help you see the biggest and most important escalations across the many levels.

Figure 2.12

Increasing Expectations for Understanding Key Details as Texts Become More Complex

---

Figure 2.13

Increasing Expectations for Understanding Vocabulary as Texts Become More Complex

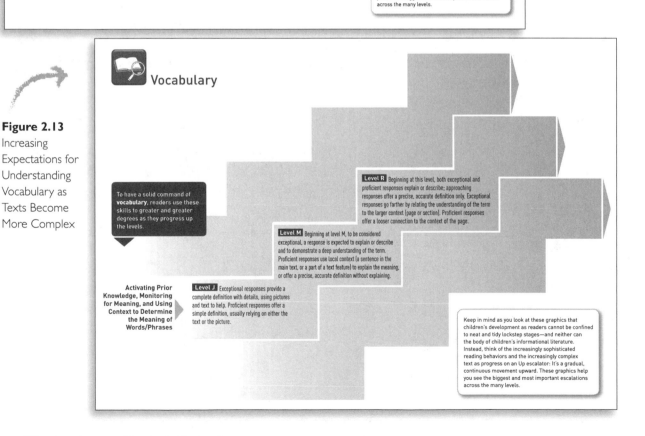

Vocabulary

To have a solid command of vocabulary, readers use these skills to greater and greater degrees as they progress up the levels.

Activating Prior Knowledge, Monitoring for Meaning, and Using Context to Determine the Meaning of Words/Phrases

Level J Exceptional responses provide a complete definition with details, using pictures and text to help. Proficient responses offer a simple definition, usually relying on either the text or the picture.

Level M Beginning at level M, to be considered exceptional, a response is expected to explain or describe and to demonstrate a deep understanding of the term. Proficient responses use local context (a sentence in the main text, or a part of a text feature) to explain the meaning, or offer a precise, accurate definition without explaining.

Level R Beginning at this level, both exceptional and proficient responses explain or describe; approaching responses offer a precise, accurate definition only. Exceptional responses go farther by relating the understanding of the term to the larger context (page or section). Proficient responses offer a looser connection to the context of the page.

Keep in mind as you look at these graphics that children's development as readers cannot be confined to neat and tidy lockstep stages—and neither can the body of children's informational literature. Instead, think of the increasingly sophisticated reading behaviors and the increasingly complex text as progress on an Up escalator: It's a gradual, continuous movement upward. These graphics help you see the biggest and most important escalations across the many levels.

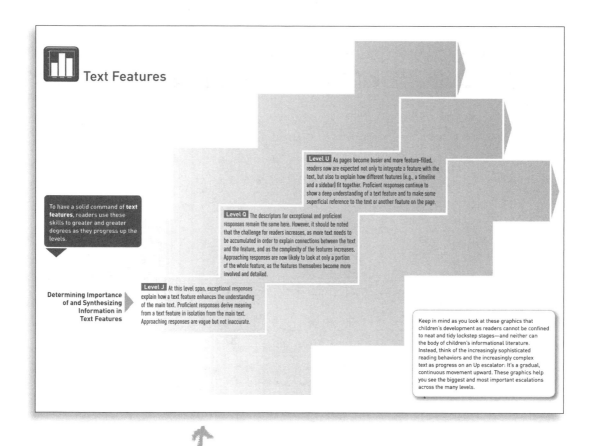

Text Features

Level U As pages become busier and more feature-filled, readers now are expected not only to integrate a feature with the text, but also to explain how different features (e.g., a timeline and a sidebar) fit together. Proficient responses continue to show a deep understanding of a text feature and to make some superficial reference to the text or another feature on the page.

Level Q The descriptors for exceptional and proficient responses remain the same here. However, it should be noted that the challenge for readers increases, as more text needs to be accumulated in order to explain connections between the text and the feature, and as the complexity of the features increases. Approaching responses are now likely to look at only a portion of the whole feature, as the features themselves become more involved and detailed.

Level J At this level span, exceptional responses explain how a text feature enhances the understanding of the main text. Proficient responses derive meaning from a text feature in isolation from the main text. Approaching responses are vague but not inaccurate.

To have a solid command of **text features,** readers use these skills to greater and greater degrees as they progress up the levels.

Determining Importance of and Synthesizing Information in Text Features

Keep in mind as you look at these graphics that children's development as readers cannot be confined to neat and tidy lockstep stages—and neither can the body of children's informational literature. Instead, think of the increasingly sophisticated reading behaviors and the increasingly complex text as progress on an Up escalator: It's a gradual, continuous movement upward. These graphics help you see the biggest and most important escalations across the many levels.

Figure 2.14 Increasing Expectations for Understanding Text Features as Texts Become More Complex

What to Look For

What to look for in a whole-book assessment varies by level. Therefore, what you see in both the "Question to Ask" and "The Ideal" columns in the chart that follows is what is important to consider for Joana's level, level R. Of course, you'll want to use what you know about characteristics of the level of books of your focus student as you consider his work. I've organized the questions—what to look for—in four strands that also align to the CCSS Reading Literature standards. For Joana, who is reading a book at level R, here are some considerations to keep in mind:

Fiction Whole-Book Comprehension Look-Fors (Level R)

Question to Ask	Where to Look	The Ideal
Plot and Setting (CCSS RL 1): What is the student's ability to describe the setting (time and place) with some original detail? What is the student's ability to connect the dots between multiple events in the story to understand cause and effect?	Responses to "Retell the most important events in this chapter" or questions and prompts such as "Describe where this scene takes place" or "What caused this even to happen?"	The student should evidence an ability to retell the most important events from a plot that is more complex, including one that has flashbacks and/or flash-forwards. A student should draw connections between multiple causes and effects to understand a scene with depth.
Character (CCSS RL 3): Can the student identify multiple traits of main and secondary characters? Does the student understand how secondary characters affect main characters? Does the student understand character change?	Answers to questions and prompts such as "Describe ____" [character name] and "How does ____ [secondary character name] affect ____ [main character name]?" and "How has ____ [character name] changed from the beginning to this point in the story?"	At this level, a student should understand that characters are complex, exhibiting several sometimes contradictory traits, and that secondary characters have an effect on main characters. A student should be able to compare a character's traits, thoughts, and/or feelings during multiple moments in a text.
Vocabulary and Figurative Language (CCSS RL 4): How is the student making sense of words and phrases that are important to the story?	Answers to questions and prompts such as "Explain what ____ means when she says ____?" and "What does ____ mean in this context?"	A student should be able to synthesize many contextual details from entire scenes or chapters to explain the meaning of the word or phrase. The student demonstrates deep understanding of event, character, or theme.

continues

Fiction Whole-Book Comprehension Look-Fors (Level R) (cont.)

Question to Ask	Where to Look	The Ideal
Themes and Ideas (CCSS RL 2): Does the child articulate a lesson or theme that can be applied to contexts outside the book, yet is grounded in the actual events of the story, including multiple plotlines? Can the student interpret symbols in the story and explain the significance of those symbols? Can the student identify and comment on social issues in the text?	Answers to questions and prompts such as "What does ___ symbolize?" and "What lesson or lessons can we learn from this story?"	The student should show she can articulate a universal lesson/theme that can be applied to other contexts outside the text, such as to other texts or the reader's own life. The student accumulates and synthesizes events from the story, taking into account multiple plotlines, and relates them to the book's lesson(s)/theme(s). The student should be able to interpret a symbol by accumulating and synthesizing several past events to explain the significance of the symbol. The child should be able to identify a social issue in the text. The student accumulates and synthesizes multiple details to explain the complexity of the issue and articulates an idea.

A Sample Analysis: Joana

Questions 2 and 6 (Figure 2.15) assess Joana's ability to track plot details and visualize setting. For both questions, she answers on a "proficient" level. She identifies the time and place, but doesn't offer her own original details. For question 6, she identifies a single connection between a past and present event, but her answer lacks complexity drawing together multiple causes and effects. She can deepen her work around plot and setting by drawing from more past events to explain the present and adding in her own original details.

Questions 1, 4, and 9 are questions that look at how well Joana can infer about characters. For questions 4 and 9 that ask about Sadako, Joana is able to offer multiple traits and explain the character in a way that offers a complex view of the character. Saying she's both "determined and confident" is an example of this. Therefore, these responses would be considered "exceptional." When asked about a secondary character, though, she tends to give a simplistic view, a "proficient" response. She doesn't yet describe the effect the secondary character has on the main character. This could be a goal for her in this area.

Questions 3, 5, 8, and 10 assess Joana's ability to determine the meaning of vocabulary and figurative language in the text. Joana does very well with this

Figure 2.15 Joana's Whole-Book Assessment

Sadako and the Thousand Paper Cranes
by Eleanor Coerr

Student Response Form

Student's name _Joana_   Grade _____ 4 _____

Your teacher wants to learn more about you as a reader. Here are some directions to remember:

- Please complete this assessment on your own. Do not ask for help or use anything (dictionaries, websites, etc.) to help you.
- Each time you read, please fill in your reading log below.
- When you reach a page with a sticky note, read to the bottom of the page.
- Stop and answer the question on your response form. Include as much detail as you can from the book to support your answer. (It is fine to reread, but do not read ahead.)
- Put the sticky note back in the book.
- Keep reading!

READING LOG

Date	Start Time	End Time	Start Page	End Page	Teacher: Please fill out.	
					Total Time	Total Pages
5/2/11	1:53	2:00	7	14		
5/4/11	10:23		15	27		
5/8/11	7:4	8:30	28	60		
5/10/11	10:05	10:21	61	79		
					Total	**59**

Sadako and the Thousand Paper Cranes
by Eleanor Coerr

1. PAGE 14 What kind of people are Sadako's family?

Some things I know about Sadako's family are that they are strickt, and don't rush.

E P A I

2. PAGE 20 Describe the setting (time and place).

The setting in this part of the story, is in the banks of the Ohto river during when it was dark. I know this because why would they light candle in the day when they can't shine?

E P A I

3. PAGE 24 What does this sentence mean: "The kind words from her parents made the knot in Sadako's stomach loosen."

The words that her parents tell her make Sadako feel less nervous about the race because they encouraged her to do her best.

E P A I

4. PAGE 27 What kind of person is Sadako?

Sadako has is a very good, kind, dot determind and confident person. I know this because in the story when she was about to raceagaints the bigger kids she won because she was confident she could. Also it says that she was determind to get into the racing team.

E P A I

Sadako and the Thousand Paper Cranes
by Eleanor Coerr

5. PAGE 32 What does leukemia mean? Use details from this part to explain the meaning.

leukemia, according to the story is the desease disease that the atom bomb spreat. Sadako asks her father if she has the disease the bomb spread.

6. PAGE 45 Explain how the moments with Kenji are important to the story.

Sadako is in the same situation as Kenji so she can better understand her future.

E P A I

7. PAGE 47 What do the cranes symbolize for Sadako?

To Sadako the cranes mean a good luck sing for her to get well. Somehow I think the paper cranes almost keep Sadako well, and not die. They make her feel more confident about having the disease and that she will get better.

8. PAGE 48 What does listless mean in this part?

I think listless means being so tired that you can't move a mustle.

E P A I

strand, as three of the four answers she gives incorporate larger story context to understand the meaning of the word or phrase. This is a real strength for her.

Joana's answers to questions 7, 11, and 12 offer us insight into how she's able to determine themes and ideas. From her answers, we can tell that Joana is very attuned to thinking of big overarching meanings in stories. She can articulate lessons, understand how to use social issues to interpret a story, and identify and interpret symbols. This is also a real strength for her.

Sadako and the Thousand Paper Cranes
by Eleanor Coerr

12. PAGE 65 What have you learned about war from reading this book?

From Sadako's story I think we can learn sometimes you have to face your troubles. You need to fight even when it seems hopeless. Sadako's story is like war.

E P A I

Reflection

Was this book easy, (just right) or too hard?

How do you know? I liked this book very much.

Did you like this book? Yes.

Why or why not? I liked it because it showed bravery and confidence.

Would you choose another book like this from the library? Yes.

Why or why not? I really understood the character and what she was going through.

Sadako and the Thousand Paper Cranes
by Eleanor Coerr

9. PAGE 59 Based on what you've read from page 27 until now, what new ideas do you have about the kind of person Sadako is?

Now I think that Sadako is a doesn't give up, even though she is sick. She always looks at the gold paper crane for hope and support. Also, she isn't giving up for trying to make 1,000 cranes.

E P A I

10. PAGE 60 Read the following line and explain what it means in this story: "But it was like trying to stop the rain from falling."

This line means that it was impossible to forget about dying because she had leukemia.

E P A I

11. PAGE 64 What lesson or lessons can we learn from Sadako's story?

War can be terrible for everyone, but especially innocent children.

E P A I

ACTION →

Pause here if you haven't already to analyze Alex's work or the work of a student from your class. Take out any work that helps you understand what your reader comprehends. If you're following along with Alex, you should take a look now at his writing about reading and perhaps the comprehension questions on his running record. You can find my thoughts about his work in Appendix A.

How I'd Summarize My Findings

Below are my summarized findings from Joana's whole-book assessment:

Tool	Strengths	Possibilities for Growth
Whole-book assessment (using *Independent Reading Assessment: Fiction* [Serravallo 2012])	• Can name the time and place • Connects significant events • Names multiple traits about main character, showing complexity • Understands meaning of unknown words and phrases, and uses context to explain • Interprets theme, social issues, and symbolism	• She could add original details when describing time and place. • She could connect several significant events. • She could name multiple traits about secondary characters to show complexity.

Excerpt from main table on pages 97–101

Analyzing a Fluency Assessment

An often-overlooked aspect of a running record is that one can also record information about a student's fluency. Often, teachers' attention is solely on recording miscues. But fluency, as many researchers have noted, has direct links to comprehension (Kuhn 2008; Rasinski 2010). In the CCSS Document, fluency has its own strand under Reading Foundational Skills (RF 4). Looking back at a running record with an eye toward fluency or recording student fluency during an oral reading and then analyzing it can be helpful.

When looking at a fluency record, we can gain insight into a student's ability to read with accuracy, expression, and phrasing. Often, these qualities of fluency are necessary precursors to a child's ability to comprehend a text. There are some rare exceptions to instances when this is true. At times, children who have processing or expressive language delays may have a particularly difficult time reading with fluency, although their comprehension is not affected. Likewise, there are some English language learners whose speech is somewhat staccato; more fluency when reading is often not possible.

When looking at child's fluency, it's important to note that a very disfluent reader is likely not matched to books properly. Aside from kindergarteners and early first graders reading at levels A to C where one-to-one matching is expected and smooth fluent reading would interfere with acquiring that new skill, a student's fluency should be around level 3 or 4 on the *National Assessment of Educational Progress (*NAEP) fluency scale (see Figure 2.16). When readers read at levels 1 or 2 on the NAEP scale, it often indicates that a reader would be better off moving to an easier text. When students are falling somewhere in level 3, it's likely that you'll set fluency as a potential goal for that student.

NAEP Oral Reading Fluency Scale

Fluent	Level 4	Reads primarily in larger, meaningful phrase groups. Although some regressions, repetitions, and deviations from text may be present, these do not appear to detract from the overall structure of the story. Presentation of the author's syntax is consistent. Some or most of the story is read with expressive interpretation.
	Level 3	Reads primarily in three- or four-word phrase groups. Some small groupings may be present. However, the majority of phrasing seems appropriate and preserves the syntax of the author. Little or no expressive interpretation is present.
Nonfluent	Level 2	Reads primarily in two-word phrases with some three- or four-word groupings. Some word-by-word reading may be present. Word groupings may seem awkward and unrelated to larger context of setting or passage
	Level 1	Reads primarily word-by-word. Occasional two-word or three-word phrases may occur—but these are infrequent and/or they do not preserve meaningful syntax.

Figure 2.16

What to Look For

When analyzing a child's fluency, you can either look at a tool like the NAEP fluency scale or look for individual qualities of fluent reading. Using the NAEP is more holistic, whereas looking at individual qualities allows you to pinpoint a possible area of need. You might ask:

Fluency Assessment Look-Fors

Question to Ask	Where to Look	The Ideal
How many words are in a phrase, on average?	Count the number of words between each pause or slash ("/") on the record.	Using appropriate syntax, the reader pauses no less often than every three to four words.
Where does the reader pause?	Look for a pause or slash on the record. Between pauses, check to see if the phrase makes sense as a phrase.	The location of the pauses maintain the author's syntax and preserve meaning.
Does the student attend to punctuation?	Look to see how you noted a child's expression during ending punctuation, such as exclamation points and question marks, and midsentence punctuation such as commas and dashes.	The student should use appropriate expression at each encounter with punctuation.
Does the student read with expression appropriate to the passage?	Look for any annotations you made about the student's expression.	The expression should match the mood or tone of the passage and/or the character's feelings within the scene.
Does the student read words automatically, or does she pause when coming across a new word to figure it out?	Look to see how frequently a pause (slash) precedes a challenging word.	Words should be automatically recognized. Working to figure out a word should happen no more than five percent of the time.

A Sample Analysis: Joana

Joana is a very fluent reader, as evidenced by the fluency record her teacher took as she listened to her oral reading of *The Van Gogh Café* (see Figure 2.17). She reads in long phrases (six to ten words) that are appropriate to the meaning of the passage and that preserve the author's syntax. She uses appropriate expression and intonation. For example, she drops her voice at the parenthesis. She pauses while reading to think, but only at appropriate spots, at the end of sentences. She is able to read words automatically, and she self-corrected when she made one error.

Joana does not need any support with fluency. She is appropriately matched to this level as an independent level text for her. She would fall in the level 4 category on the NAEP fluency scale.

How I'd Summarize My Findings

To summarize my findings about Joana's fluency, I'd say:

Tool	Strengths	Possibilities for Growth
Fluency (from running record)	• Appropriate phrasing • Matches the intonation to the meaning in the text • Automaticity • Attends to punctuation	N/A
		Excerpt from main table on pages 97–101

Running Record Miscue Analysis

A running record is a helpful tool to quickly notice three aspects of a reader: the strategies a student uses to figure out unknown words; how fluently a student can read; whether a student can comprehend a text on a basic level. We've already discussed what to look for in terms of fluency and comprehension; you should apply that knowledge when analyzing a running record. This section will discuss miscue analysis, or finding out what students do when they encounter unknown words in texts.

I find running records essential for students reading levels A to J. At those levels, having an eye on word-solving strategies is essential. By the time students get to chapter books, running records might be one tool you use, but it shouldn't be the only one. Whole-book assessments of student comprehension and/or other informal snapshots of a student's thinking in a whole text (such as the read-aloud stop-and-jot assessment described in Chapter 1) are also essential.

Running record miscue analysis is very involved and can be quite complex. Entire books are written about it! In this section, I give you some basic information to help you get started, but if you teach students who read at levels A to J, I encourage you to treat this as merely an introduction and seek out some of the work of Marie Clay, such as her book on running records published by Heinemann in 2000.

You may also consult the CCSS Reading Foundational (RF) Skills document, which addresses the sorts of Print Concepts (RF 1) and Phonics and Word Recognition (RF 3) that is expected by grade level. Of course, many of the types of things we expect students to do in these areas also relate to the level of text at which they are reading. For example, you wouldn't expect a child reading on level C to know the word *because* as a sight word. To learn what to expect students to be able to do at each level, any of Fountas and Pinnell's materials are good resources (i.e., *Guided Reading*, 1996; *Benchmark Assessment System*, 2010, and so on).

Remember from Chapter 1 that analyzing an instructional-level running record yields the most information, as there are more opportunities to observe the student's problem-solving behaviors.

What to Look For

When performing a miscue analysis on a running record, you make your best inference about what was happening in a student's brain when he encountered the unfamiliar word. There is no way to know for sure, but we know that proficient readers tend to use three cueing systems: meaning (or semantic information), structure (or syntactical information), and/or visual (graphophonic information).

Using all three cueing systems allows a proficient reader to read a word that matches the meaning of the text, sounds right syntactically, and matches the letters of the word. Students who are learning to read will encounter difficulty in a text and need to work to figure out the word. Their process, and the cueing systems they use, will then become visible.

To analyze a miscue, read up to (but not beyond) the error. Ask yourself three questions to determine if the student used one, two, three, or none of the cueing systems:

- Does the error make sense?
- Does the error sound right?
- Does the error look right?

When students use the *meaning* cueing system, the word they read in error still makes sense with what's happening in the story. A student needs to use knowledge of the story/text so far, as well as any information from the pictures (if there are any). It's possible that the error doesn't mean the same thing as the word in the text, but that you could still say the student used meaning. For example, if the text says "I put the *sauce* on my sandwich" and the actual text says "I put the *ketchup* on my sandwich," that error makes sense but doesn't mean the exact same thing. Likewise, "I put the *mustard* on my sandwich" makes sense, but doesn't mean the exact same thing.

When students use the *structure* cueing system, the word they read in error sounds syntactically appropriate in the sentence. Often, it's the same part of speech as the word in the text. Both of the examples above—*mustard* or *sauce* instead of *ketchup*—would be syntactically correct because they are nouns. It's possible for a word to not make sense but still be syntactically correct, and vice versa.

When students use the *visual* cueing system, the word they read in error has some of the same letters or sounds in common as the word in the text. Often, students look first at the initial letter or cluster of letters, next at the end of the word, and finally at the middle of the word. Sauce and mustard do not *look right* because they do not share the same beginning, ending, or middle letters as *ketchup*, the word in the text.

In the instance of a self-correction, you might ask yourself those three questions to analyze the miscue, and then ask yourself those three questions again to analyze the self-correction. In other words, did the student use meaning, syntax, and/or visual to fix his reading of the word?

Once you've analyzed each miscue separately, look across the errors to see if you can determine a pattern. I ask myself:

Running Record Look-Fors

Question to Ask	Where to Look	The Ideal
What does the student tend to use when encountering an unknown word?	Look at your analysis of all of the miscues. Count up the number of times the student uses meaning, syntax, and visual.	The student use all three cueing systems together. What you might find, however, is a tendency to use one or two of the systems. A student might also use one or two at first, and then cross-check using one or two of the others.
When the student self-corrects, what cueing systems most likely helped him to self-correct?	Look at your analysis of all of the self-corrections. Count up the number of times the student uses meaning, syntax, and visual to self-correct.	The fact that the student is self-correcting at all is very encouraging. The ideal is a high self-correction rate (that is, almost any time the student makes an error she corrects it). It's interesting to analyze which system the student uses because teaching a student to use this when first encountering a word could help the miscue rate decrease.

continues

Running Record Look-Fors (cont.)

Question to Ask	Where to Look	The Ideal
What cueing system(s) is the child not using consistently?	Look at your analysis of all of the miscues. Count up the number of times the student uses meaning, syntax, and visual.	Ideally the student uses all three, but if you find that there is one or two that are not being used, then teaching the student to use them together with the most often used cueing system could help to decrease the error rate.

I must be careful, as always, to not look for a deficit, but instead for possibility. I look to see what a child is doing inconsistently that might be helpful for him to do all the time. I look to see what the student's strength is so that I can lean on that strength to support the area of need.

A Sample Analysis: Joana

Joana's performance on this running record (Figure 2.17) is typical for readers in grades 4 and above, sometimes even at grade 3. It's often the case that a student reading at these higher levels makes very few miscues. Sometimes, readers can even read with incredibly high accuracy, well above the level at which they read independently with comprehension.

From this running record, we can't glean much about the word-solving strategies she uses. And truthfully, word solving is probably not what Joana needs the most help with anyway. Keep in mind, also, that this running record is at Joana's independent, not instructional, level. Remember there is a limit to the information you can glean when the accuracy rate is very high. Be sure that you conduct *instructional-level* running records to get the most benefit from your miscue analysis.

In terms of comprehension, this running record gives us just a snapshot since it's a several-hundred-word excerpt of a longer text. What we can determine is that Joana is able to summarize some of the most basic information from a story. Her retelling offers just a gist—telling about the main events and the characters' feelings about the main events.

Her answers to the comprehension questions are correct, if brief. Her answer to the third question shows that she is aware of nonliteral language, which shows her skills of inference are strong. It is particularly impressive that she isn't tripped up by figurative language given that she's an English language learner.

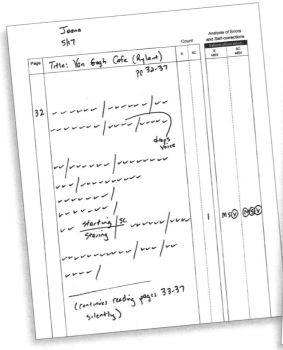

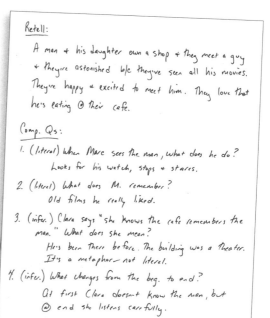

Figure 2.17 Joana's Running Record

Running Record Sheet © 2005 by Marie M. Clay from *An Observation Survey of Early Literacy Achievement*, Third Edition (2013). Published by Pearson, a division of Pearson New Zealand Ltd. Reprinted by permission of the author's estate.

How I'd Summarize My Findings

Here is a summary of my conclusions about Joana's running record:

Tool	Strengths	Possibilities for Growth
Running record	• Successfully uses all three cueing systems • Reads accurately and automatically • Retells correctly, briefly • Answers comprehension questions correctly, briefly • Understands words used figuratively	• She could elaborate during retell and when answering comprehension questions.

Excerpt from main table on pages 97–101

ACTION →

Practice a miscue analysis. If you're using Alex's work, take a look at his running record. Analyze miscues as well as fluency. Find out my thinking about his running record in Appendix A.

Analyzing Conversation

When you go back to look at a transcript, listen to a recording, or watch a video of your students' conversation in a book club or partnership, it's helpful to tune in with two lenses in mind. You might be thinking about their abilities to articulate their thinking about the text, *and* you might be thinking about their speaking and listening skills.

Often, it's hard to get everything on just the first look, watch, or listen. That's part of what makes conferring during conversation so difficult—you need to be able to listen, think, and make a decision in the moment. Going back to a recording of the conversation allows you time to revisit the conversation again and again to get all you can from the sample of student work. Looking at a transcript, like the one I have included in this book for Joana (Figure 2.18), allows you to read, process, and think about the student's conversational skills at your own pace.

What to Look For

When looking at a transcript for the first time, or listening to a conversation, it is important to think about the student's abilities in terms of speaking and listening. The CCSS's Speaking and Listening strand has some helpful insights, organized by grade level, about what to expect of students. The Comprehension and Collaboration standards (Standards 1 and 2), are most helpful for the type of analysis in this section.

When considering speaking and listening skills, you might ask yourself:

Conversation Look-Fors

Question to Ask	Where to Look	The Ideal
Does the student actively participate in the conversation?	Compare the amount of time each student spends speaking.	There is balance in terms of who is speaking and how much each is saying; in other words, no single student dominates the conversation.

continues

Conversation Look-Fors (cont.)

Question to Ask	Where to Look	The Ideal
Is the student able to offer ideas that follow the main topic of conversation?	When the student speaks, look to see if what she says relates to what the person before her said.	The student should be able to stay on topic.
Is the student able to build on another student's ideas, deepening the thought, not just repeating the thought?	Compare what the student says to what the person or people before her said. Look to see if it is the same thing in different words.	Ideally the student is contributing new or deeper thoughts to the conversation.
Does the student use appropriate behaviors during the conversation?	Watch the student's body language during the conversation.	The student should look at the speaker, waiting respectfully for a turn. Natural interjections and interruptions are a great sign of organic conversation, but rudely speaking over others is not.
What does the student do when an idea is offered that differs from his own?	Look for a moment when a member of the conversation offers an idea that differs from the child whose conversation you're evaluating. See what the student does next.	The student should be able to "try on" another student's ideas, grappling with a thought that wasn't initially her own. Perhaps the student looks for evidence to support the other student's ideas, or ask clarifying questions in an effort to better understand where the other student is coming from.
Does the student reference text appropriately during book talks?	Look to see if the student references the text by either opening up the book and reading from it, paraphrasing something from the text, or reading from notes he has written.	The book needs to be in the book talk. Children should be encouraged to discuss details from the text along with their own thoughts and reactions from the text.

The second time you read the transcript or listen to the conversation, you can also think about comprehension. Everything a student says reveals something about his understanding about the text.

- Does the student offer ideas during the conversation that are based on an accurate understanding of the text?
- Which of the reading comprehension thinking strategies does the student use, and how deep is the use of each (see section on stop-and-jots, pages 40–46)?
- How well is the student doing the work of the level (see section on whole-book comprehension, pages 46–56)?

S3: I think the theme of this book is don't judge a book by its cover because Crash sort of judged Penn in the beginning when he just moved in when they were in first grade and the end, the last line of the book is, "Penn Webb is my best friend." So I think that's a big theme.

Joana: Another theme is that friends can come from unexpected people. I remember doing a theme web and adding the book *Crash* to it because Crash, at first he's like . . . well, he . . . Penn tries to be his friend but Crash kind of like . . .

S3: He acts too tough for him . . .

Joana: Yeah. And like . . .

S3: In the end he softens . . .

Joana: Yeah. He becomes more sensitive and understands that Penn has been trying to be his friend but he just ignores him.

S2: Well, I agree with you, but I think it's not don't judge a book by its cover but maybe don't judge other people by their backgrounds because Penn came from North Dakota and . . .

S3: Or, he's a vegetarian . . .

S2: Yeah, he's a vegetarian. And . . .

Joana: And a Quaker . . .

S3: Yeah, but also they thought he looked weird because remember he wore buttons sometimes and stuff like that? So, he could look weird too. So, don't judge a book by its cover.

Figure 2.18 Transcript of Joana's Conversation

Teacher: Can I interrupt you for a minute? I think this is really great that you're think-ing and talking about the big ideas in the stories, about the themes in the stories. I don't want to interrupt you for too long but I just wanted to ask you if you could think about theme as being something that's not just necessarily about the main plotline or about the main character, but sometimes in a book the author will craft it in such a way that theme goes across multiple storylines. Right? So in this book, think about different relationships and if you learn the same lesson from both of those relationships. Or different main events in the story and if you learn the same lesson from the different main events in the story. Are you thinking something?

S4: Well, when Crash is not around Mike, who is his friend but is really rough and mean . . . Like, let's say, at home with his sister, he felt bad for his sister so he made the cake. But when he's with Mike he acts tough and rough and mean and bullyish and he just totally changes his character.

Teacher: So what's the theme you are thinking about from both of those?

S4: That Crash is sensitive but . . . I think his real side is sensitive because Mike, it's just when Crash is around Mike. When Crash is not around Mike, and around every-thing else but not in school, he's the person he really is, which is sensitive and kind, not at all like Mike.

Joana: Well, what do you say, like what's the theme, not like what the character is?

S4: Mike is a really bad influence because he is an actual bully. Crash just like learns from Mike . . .

Teacher: So that's very book specific, but if you want to say it like a theme you have to say it in a universal way, to the world.

Joana: So what you're saying is that one person can have two different sides and can be influenced by two different people.

S4: Yeah.

S3: Like two-faced? Like, sometimes they call a person two-faced because sometimes they're acting sensitive and sometimes they act tough around other people.

Teacher: So what I am trying to get you guys to do . . . that's a great job of saying it in a world way or a universal way, "Sometimes people can be two-faced." What I'm trying to get you to do is to come up with, together, a theme that goes for more than one character or goes for more than one plotline. So, people can be two-faced. Is that true with another character in the story?

[Girls shake their heads.]

continues

Teacher: Not really. OK. So let's think of another theme and let's try it out and see if we can think of how it goes with more than one thing in the book. Either more than one plot or more than one character. Who's got another idea?

S2: Well, I think that Penn is also sensitive. So he kind of shares the same thing as Crash. Even though, I think he covers it up, because he seems to be a little affected when Crash brags and lies about how he has great-, great-, great-grand-parents when Penn is already proud that he has a great-grandparent. And I think Crash just ruins his pride by lying.

Teacher: And that's similar to what else in the story?

S2: Well, I think it's also similar to how they act. Because in this story I think they always influence each other. Abby's influenced by Penn about the mall and Crash is influenced by Mike.

S4: Sort of how they interact with each character?

S3: Relationships and friends . . . like the influence, it bounces off somebody to another person to influence them. Just like Mike influenced Crash but it's not always in a good way.

S4: I agree with you.

Joana: You know, I just got the idea of a theme that could be for the whole book. You know there are so many. It kind of goes with all plots and with what you were saying about friendships that kind of influence and bounce off. So maybe the theme is that friends can influence you in affected ways. Like Mike affects Crash and makes him bully Penn. And, like you were saying, Abby kind of takes the influ-ence from Penn, so it's like . . .

S3: So, you're saying that relationships influence people, but not always in a good way.

Joana: Yeah.

S4: Cool, yeah.

S2: I kind of think that Jane Forbes was influenced by Penn and she didn't like the way that Mike and Crash were acting, but she liked the way that Penn was acting. And I could agree with her because . . . I think groups formed and they kind of became separated. Jane Forbes, Penn Webb, and Abby in a group, and then Crash in a group . . .

> **Teacher:** So, let me stop you guys. I'll let you keep talking, but that's the idea. Because sometimes you can talk about a theme, and it's true, you could interpret one part of the story or one character in a certain way. But when you find that theme that matches with all the different characters, or matches with all the different plotlines then you have a lot to talk about as a club. And you can keep talking and talking and talking. So it's fun work to do this with your club. To come with . . . if you all have in your notebooks a bunch of different ideas of what some possible themes or interpretations of the story could be and share them out and see if you can find multiple characters or multiple plots that fit with that same idea. Alright? Keep talking. Nice work guys.

A Sample Analysis: Joana

Joana is extremely polite and patient in this conversation. She exhibits behaviors that prove she's an active participant in a conversation—facing the speaker, listening intently, waiting her turn. There are a couple of times in this conversation when another student spoke for, or on top of, Joana, and a time when she is trying to get a word in edgewise. It might be worth it to teach her to try to be a little bolder in order to help her ideas be heard (and to teach her book club members to notice when someone is trying to speak!)

One impressive thing about Joana in this conversation is how she is able to listen carefully to others' ideas, sort through them, and synthesize them. She easily takes on the teaching I do, and her participation brings the club's conversation to a slightly deeper level.

She supports her ideas with textual evidence, showing that her ideas are very grounded in the book. She is able to interpret (theme) by stating it in a universal way, and she juggles multiple plots and characters in articulating why that theme is one to consider.

How I'd Summarize My Findings

After rereading the transcript of Joana's conversation with her book club, I'd summarize my interpretations as follows:

Tool	Strengths	Possibilities for Growth
Conversation transcript	• Polite and patient, follows agreed-upon rules for discussion • Listens carefully to sort through and synthesize others' ideas • Supports ideas with text evidence • Interprets theme • Takes into account multiple plots and characters	• She could advocate for herself more in conversation to allow her ideas to be heard.

Excerpt from main table on pages 97–101

ACTION ➞

- Take a look at the notes from one of Alex's partnership conversations, or from the conversation of the student you're studying. What do you notice?
- This concludes the reading section. If you've collected student work or have other assessments you'd like to consider to better understand your student as a reader, now's the time to take a look at those. As you do, consider the type of information you can glean from each piece of work and use the appropriate tables in the preceding sections to help you. If you find that the student work sample you're looking at doesn't actually help you that much to learn about the student, consider eliminating that type of work/ assessment from your repertoire. If you're working with Alex's work, you should have analyzed his running record, writing about reading, reading log, and conversation. Remember that you can look at my analysis in Appendix A.

Making Discoveries from Narrative Writing

Narrative writing is an umbrella term that incorporates a variety of types of writing. Narrative writing is any type of writing in which a writer attempts to tell a story, often with a sequence of events. Narrative writing often has a plot, characters, a setting, and, in the most sophisticated examples, an overarching theme.

To use the advice in this section, you should have in front of you an example of a student's personal narrative, realistic fiction, fantasy, historical fiction, or some other type of genre fiction. Personal narrative is a type of writing in which a writer attempts to tell a story about himself. At the Teachers College Reading and Writing Project, we call a personal narrative that is very focused in time a "small moment" narrative. Some memoir can be considered a "personal narrative" as well, as long as the memoir has a narrative structure.

In the CCSS document, grade-level expectations for narrative writing are under Writing Standard 3.

What to Look For

With any piece of writing, I find it helpful to look at both qualities of good writing and writing process.

I find it most helpful to think through each of the qualities of good writing mentioned first in Chapter 1. Here I give you a series of guiding questions aligned to each quality of good writing to help focus your analysis. You may also consult the CCSS, which gives information about what to expect, by grade level.

Focus refers to the writer's ability to focus a piece in time or by meaning. For example, some writers might write all about their summer vacation. Others might write just about the week at their grandmother's house. One might write about the day they went to Great Adventure, and still another would focus the piece just on the roller-coaster ride. In general, a more focused piece is harder to pull off because the greater the focus, the more the writer needs to elaborate.

When focusing by meaning, a writer must consider "What is it that I'm trying to show about myself?" (if the writing is a personal narrative) or "What idea/message/lesson am I trying to communicate?" about other types of fiction. Refer to CCSS Writing 3.a and 3.e for grade-level expectations. After reading the entire narrative, you may ask yourself:

Narrative Writing Look-Fors: Focus

Question to Ask	Where to Look	The Ideal
Does that amount of time seem to serve the purpose/ meaning of the story, or would a narrative more focused in time or expanded in time be better?	Notice the beginning, middle, and end of the piece, asking yourself how much time passes during this story.	The amount of time that passes in the story should match the child's intended meaning. For example, to show the excitement of a first ride on a roller coaster, it's not necessary to write about what she had for breakfast, the game she played in the car, and brushing her teeth before bed. Unless all of those events are imbued with a sense of buildup and anticipation for the event.
Is there a central idea that focuses the piece?	After reading the story, try to articulate a message, lesson, or idea.	Students should have some purpose for telling the story they chose to tell.
How well is the central idea maintained throughout the entire story?	Look at how a student uses details such as a character's inner thinking to give hints about the message. Look to see if each part of the story relates back to the overarching message.	The student should be able to focus the piece, disregarding details or parts of the story that aren't aligned to the overall point of the story.

Structure refers to how a piece is organized. Consider in narrative if the piece is organized in a linear fashion or if the writer plays with the order of events (i.e., flashback and flash-forward). Think about the pacing of the narrative overall. You may also consider the structure within the parts—the beginning, middle, and end. Refer to CCSS Writing 3.a and 3.e for grade-level expectations.

Narrative Writing Look-Fors: Structure

Question to Ask	Where to Look	The Ideal
Is there a sequence of events in the story that makes it easy to follow and understand?	Try to create a timeline from the events of the story. See if one event leads logically to the next.	A reader should be clear on how one event leads to another. Young writers have a tendency to leave events out, assuming the reader possesses the same knowledge about the events as the writer.
Are all of the events in the narrative given equal treatment, or does the writer play with speeding some events up and slowing some down?	Draw a mental box around each event in the narrative, noticing the length of each.	The amount of time given to each event relates to the meaning in the piece. Often, this means that the "heart of the story"—or the story that contains the most important meaning—is the longest.
Does the writer use flashbacks or flash-forwards? If used, how effective are they?	Notice if each event follows in sequence or if some events give glimpses into what will happen later in the story, or if a character thinks back to a time that precedes the time described in the story.	If flashbacks or flash-forwards are used, they should match the meaning and/or tone of the piece.
How strong is the story's beginning?	Look at the first paragraph or so of the story.	The beginning should capture the reader's attention, inviting the reader into the story.
Does the story have good closure?	Read the final paragraph or final event.	The closure is an opportunity for the author to reiterate the main message of the story.

Elaboration refers to the details in a story. Consider the types of details the writer uses and how well that detail is used. Novice writers tend to write with very sparse details, breezing by important events, or to flood their writing with lots of detail without meaning or purpose. Refer to CCSS Writing 3.b, 3.c, and 3.d for grade-level-specific expectations.

Narrative Writing Look-Fors: Elaboration

Question to Ask	Where to Look	The Ideal
Does the writer use any of the following types of detail: setting, character description or development, action, narration, internal thinking?	Sentence by sentence, notice the types of details the student uses to develop his piece.	There should be a balance of types of detail.
How well is each type of detail used?	Sentence by sentence, consider if the details support the meaning.	Details should help to communicate the meaning in the piece. Extra details that don't help develop the meaning should be cut.
Is the writer able to draw out events with a lot of detail and proceed through less important events with less detail?	Look part by part to see if the amount of detail used within a part matches the importance of the part.	More important parts are developed with more detail, less important parts are written with more spare language.

Conventions refers to the writer's ability to use grammar and punctuation in a way that aids in the meaning of the piece. The CCSS give very precise advice in the Language Standards strand about what conventions students should have control of by the end of each grade level. Keep in mind that our goal is not always to have writing be conventionally perfect—there are many instances of published writers who write one-word sentences or one-sentence paragraphs. They do so not out of a lack of awareness, but rather because that "breaking of the rules" has an effect and matches the meaning of the piece (Ehrenworth and Vinton 2005; Feigelson 2008). Consider:

Narrative Writing Look-Fors: Conventions

Question to Ask	Where to Look	The Ideal
What does the student understand about spelling?	Take note of the types of words the student tends to spell incorrectly and those the child spells correctly. See if you can notice a pattern about the features of the words (e.g., vowel blends, multisyllabic words, words with inflected endings).	The student has a strong sense of how words work. Errors are infrequent and when they do occur they do not dramatically affect readability.
What does the student understand about sentence structure?	Take note of the types and varieties of sentences the writer includes within the piece (e.g., fragments, run-ons, compound, complex, simple, and so on).	Sentence structure is varied and matches the purpose and meaning of the piece (e.g., using a fragment to communicate a halt in thinking or actions).
What does the student understand about punctuation?	Look for how the child uses punctuation, both correctly and incorrectly.	This child knows how to use conventionally correct punctuation. When the writer "breaks a rule," it seems to be done purposefully for an effect.

In addition to the qualities of good writing of an on-demand or published piece of writing, it's also important to consider a child's writing *process*. If you have examples of notebook entries and/or drafts, you can look at those in an attempt to understand something about that child's process, as well as his *engagement* and *stamina* when it comes to writing. Consider:

Process, Engagement, and Stamina Look-Fors

Question to Ask	Where to Look	The Ideal
How would you describe the student's volume of writing?	Count how many pages a child tends to fill in a given day—both at home and at school. Notice if volume increases across the year.	It should appear that the student spends at least forty-five minutes a day writing. In that time, the student produces several pages of writing. Writing pace varies from student to student and among children of different ages. Writing volume should increase across the year.
Does the student have a process?	See if you can follow a child's process from the notebook to the draft to the published piece. If the student works in a writing workshop, the prewriting (brainstorming, choosing, and planning) will probably happen in a writer's notebook, whereas the drafting, revising, and editing will likely happen on draft paper outside of the notebook.	It should be clear that the student does some prewriting/brainstorming, chooses a topic, plans out his writing, drafts, and then revises and edits before making the piece final. Ideally, the writing will change with each iteration showing the process helps the writer to rethink his work.

A Sample Analysis: Joana
Qualities of Good Writing

Looking at Joana's narrative writing (Figure 2.19), it's clear that she understands that a story needs to have a point—she does work in her notebook and in the final piece to explore the story's message or theme. She does a good job of focusing her scenes to develop that message. At times her details overexplain the message to her reader, but this can be expected for a nine-year-old.

The structure of her story is logical and sequential. She attempts to build suspense at the end of chapters. The resolution of the story seems to come quickly and not entirely realistically (over a plate of cookies a bully begins to feel remorseful) but she does have an understanding of how a story needs to have a beginning, a middle, and an end.

The New Girl

by Joana

Chapter 1

I ran as fast as I could down the steep hill as the wind broke on my face and sweat trickled down my neck like rain drops sliding down from a roof. From here I could hear the excited yells from my school as the teachers tried to calm down the first day excitement. As I slowed down I could see the black bars that surrounded the whole school and smell the fresh paint that was coming from the bars. Finally after a few minutes I reached the school yard. It was full and crowded with crying kids and happy parents . Slowly I approached another girl from my class. She was too busy talking to her friends to notice me coming, so that made me really mad. I poked her hard as I could with my index finger. That got her attention! She turned to protest but she

1.

stopped when she saw me standing behind her. Her face went completely white. "Hi Madeline" I said a litte too sweetly. "Having a good time on your first day of shool?" I continued. I was loving this! "Oh, umm, hhi-hi Jenny" she stuttered. I smirked at her and walked away. If you thought the yard was crowded you should have seen the hallways. Teachers were

rushing around getting ready their classrooms and kids from older grades running around pushing little kids out of the way. As I rushed to my classroom I thought about who my next victim was going to be. Way back in second grade when I was swinging on the swings when some older kids came up to me and pushed me the ground. "Get out of our way baby" one of them said. Since then I learned that if I was going to survive school I had to stand up for myself. So now I made people feel bad about themselves. The best thing about that is that it kind of made me the boss of them. Suddenly my teachers voice brought me from my thoughts. "So, Janie could you tell us more about yourself?"asked Ms. Davis. The girl on her right shook her head furiously. I could see the girls anxious face liß she desperately wanted to hide behind a desk. She wore rag jeans and had a plain blue hoodie on. Her face was beet red

like a tomato."Ugh, who put her in here" I thought. Our eyes made contact but I quickly looked away. The new girl. She would make the perfect victim! This was going to be good...

2

Chapter 2

"Rrrrriiiiiiiiiinngggggggg" the bell rang as I tried to keep the sound out of my ears as some of the student stormed out of the room for recess. But I wasn't in a rush. I had some other things I needed to work on. I ran to the tool shelf and got some white lined paper, scotch tape and a black sharpie. On the paper I wrote in bold capital letters "**PINCH ME**" and stuck some tape on it . Then I ran outside and scanned the yard. There she was sitting alone on that bench! Now was my chance! I skipped to her quietly and patted her gently while sticking the paper on her back."Hiya Janie,

3

what's up?" I asked her. "Hi" she whispered, "um"- but I cut her off. Then I pinched her. "Oww, why did you do that for?" she asked rubbing her arm. Really loudly I yelled " Well duh! "There is a pinch me sign on your back". Some people heard me and they purposely walked by her and pinched her. This might have been my best

PINCH ME!

5

prank so far! She gasped and turned around to see it. Then she tried to take it off, but she couldn't reach it. She ran around the yard but it was no use. One by one everyone came to pinch her. See I told you they would do anything I did. I wasn't pinching her anymore because I was too busy laughing! Unfortunately the recess bell rang so everyone had to come inside. But that did not stop the pinching. Finally I saw Janie quickly sneak over to the bathroom, so gleefully I yelled "Hey, there she is hiding in the bathroom!" Some people rushed over to the bathroom. Suddenly something really fast came sprinting from the bathroom. Then I

6

Soon the girls bathroom was about to burst! ~~Suddenly something really fast came sprinting from the bathroom.~~ Then I noticed it was Janie. Her eyes were big, red and puffy so, I figured she had been crying. Then she did something that surprised me: She pushed me as hard as she could on the floor. The pain spread through my body as quickly as I got up. But I couldn't see Janie anymore...

7

Chapter 3

Even though I got detention after school it was worth it. As I closed in on my street I could smell chocolate chip cookies coming from my house! I ran inside and was greeted by my mom holding a huge tray of chocolate chip cookies in my face. " First day of school snack!"she yelled. My mouth watered as I took one from the plate. I hadn't realized I was this hungry. " Thanks mom,you are the best" I said as I inhaled another cookie. I took the plate from my mom's hands and ran upstairs to my room. There I took out a book and started reading it. Reading a book always cleared her mind.

8   9

Figure 2.19 Joana's Realistic Fiction Story

continues

After while of reading I put my book down. Now I realized how mean what I did to Janie was. She hadn't done anything wrong expect try to be my friend and I had repaid her with that mean trick. If I were her I wouldn't feel bad about pushing me. I had deserved that. Now I understood that taking those mean kids who pushed me from the swing as an example was a bad choice. You had to treat others the way you wanted them to treat you. What had I done? By now I had finished the whole plate of cookies and realized how long I had been sitting there. As I said, reading always cleared up my mind. " Honey, its dinner time!""Come and get it!"she called. I stood up and barely dragged myself down the

stairs. I barely ate my dinner and when I went to bed I could not sleep at all. I did not know that this could affect me so much. Finally I got some sleep. The next

day when my mom called me to get up I was so startled I almost fell out of bed. "I'm coming" I called. I ate some breakfast and put on a jacket. Then I stormed out the door with a quick good bye to my mom, and ran as fast as I could to my school to find Janie.

When I arrived in the schoolyard I desperately searched for Janie. I needed to

find her and tell her I am sorry or I would never forgive myself. Finally a lot of looking I spotted her sitting in her line spot. I saw her look in my direction, but she quickly looked away into another direction. That's when I realized how nervous I was right this moment. I slowly approached her. She pretended not to see me. This was going to be harder than I thought. "HEY, Janie" "Look, I am so, so, so sorry for what I did and I shouldn't have done it and I am sorry again" I said. "Do you forgive me?" I asked.

A few seconds passed before she answered. "It is okay, I got over it". But it didn't seem like she had gotten over it. Her hair was a birds nest her eyes were red and she bags under them.

"Friends?" I asked. "Friends" she replied and we gave each other a high five! I guess that was a sign for friendship...

End

BEST FRIENDS!!!

Everybody in school thinks Jenny is the meanest girl in town. She played unpleasant tricks on everybody that got in her way and everyone was scared of her. But everything changes when Janie moves in her class. Jenny is determined to make her school time miserable. Crazy things happen during the time she figures out how she has acted. Can a new girl change everything?

An entertaining book!
-The New York times

Joana uses a blend of different types of detail. She uses action to move the plot forward, inner thinking to develop the thoughts and feelings of her characters, and dialogue to show relationships between characters and move the plot along. She is clearly trying out "show, not tell" but she does a lot of telling the reader what to be thinking and learning about the characters, too. She seems to have a strong command of being able to slow down the action and tell a story with a lot of elaboration.

Joana achieves voice in her writing by varying sentence structure and length. See, for example, the beginning of Chapter 2. Some of her sentences may be considered a run-on as she is trying to include a great deal of elaboration within many of her sentences (i.e., not just what happened and who did it, but how it happened and alongside what other events and in what setting). Joana is an English language learner (she has lived in Germany, Albania, and Greece) and at times some grammatical misunderstandings come through. For example, when she writes "Why did you do that for?" instead of "What did you do that for?" These errors are rare, however. She uses ending punctuation, commas, quotation marks correctly fairly consistently throughout the book.

Process

Figure 2.20 shows several entries from Joana's writer's notebook. Joana's realistic fiction writing shows that she follows a process. On May 10 in her notebook, she brainstormed a list of possible topics from "big moments" in her own life. On May 11, she tried thinking of social issues like fitting in and bullying and letting that inspire some story ideas. She chose an idea about the bully, Ester. On May 16 and 17, she did some writing about her purpose, or what it was she's trying to show through her story. On May 18, she spent time developing her characters, and on May 25, she began placing her characters in scenes. On May 31, she planned the leads to her story before drafting. You can draw a direct line from some of these early entries to her published piece. One of her strengths is that she doesn't just copy from the notebook to the draft—she sees every step in the process as an opportunity for revision.

Her volume of writing is strong, and it's clear that she writes in school and often at home. Her volume increases across the year. These are indicators of good writing engagement.

As her teacher's staff developer, I am fully aware of the plans for the unit of study and I can tell what day each lesson was taught. Joana tends to do exactly as told—she dutifully goes back and tries out the teaching point. While this may be a dream for many teachers, Joana is a strong writer who may benefit from taking some risks. I wonder how much of the teaching is internalized, how much of it she really *owns* as a writer, or if she simply follows the steps her teacher provides.

5/10

BIG moments in my life...

* · first day going horse-back riding
· moving from Albania to New York.
· My tenth birthday
· the day my brother was born
· going to camp in Greece being the youngest person there
· going ice skating at city ice pavillon, Bryant Park and rockafeller center.
· Going to a ~~Greece~~ Greek island and going fishing for the first time.

I could write a story about a girl named Isabella who loved to ride horses. She had entered or a ~~race~~ horse-back riding race and she is determind to win. She Has a best friend who is supporting and helping her practice for the race. Isabella is 10 years old and lives in a farm and has some horses in her stable. Horses name: Snowflake. (names)

Figure 2.20 Joana's Narrative Notebook Entries

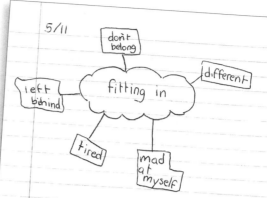

5/11

fitting in
don't belong
different
left behind
tired
mad at myself

I could write a story about a boy who didn't know englisht and was having trouble making friends. Even when he learned the language he didn't have many friends. He always sat alone at lunch and he was never noticed. He was always picked last in gym. ~~Then one boy~~ He always felt different, and like he didn't belong here.

5/16

I could write a story about a story about a girl named Ester who is a good student and teachers pet. but is a bully to the new girl. She is a pupolar girl, dresses nice, gets good grades and judges other people by what they look like not by the content of their character. She is bullying the new girl because she wears rag clothes and doesn't have a tv!

Purpose: My purpose was to show and teach the reader that you shouldn't judge someone by what they look like but by the content of their character.

5/17

I am thinking that I really want to show how... my main character understand that she shouldn't judge people by what they look like but by the content of their character... so... I could show how she acts all sweet around the teachers and her friends but not so sweet to the new girl.

Or I could show how... many pranks she pulls on the new girl and how the new girl is getting highly humiliated because of the pranks and doesn't tell the teachers of the hard time she is having.

Actually, maybe it could be that I am telling the story from the new girls point of view and see how it would change the whole story. It would talk about how the new girls feelings were about the popular girl and how she treated the new girl. That way I could be showing my purpose... that you shouldn't judge someone by what they look like but by the content of their character.

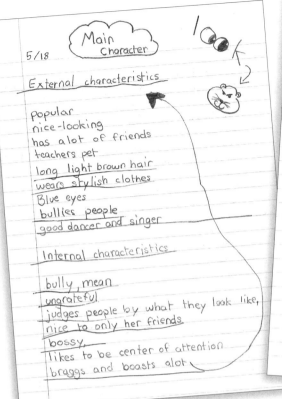

5/18

Main Character

External characteristics

popular
nice-looking
has a lot of friends
teachers pet
long light brown hair
wears stylish clothes
Blue eyes
bullies people
good dancer and singer

Internal characteristics

bully, mean
ungrateful
judges people by what they look like,
nice to only her friends
bossy,
likes to be center of attention
braggs and boasts alot

5/25

"Come on, Honey you are going to be late for school if you don't hurry up!" called my mom. I sprinted outside without saying good bye to my mom. It was the first day of school and I was way to tired to hear her tell me the rules. After a few minutes I'm standing at the ~~plag~~ playground, shivering from the soft breeze. Sweat trickled down my neck as I approached my friends. I wondered if they still wanted to be my friends. But then I shook that thought away. I was the most popular girl in the 4th grade. I was like a legend. I enjoyed bullying other kids because in second grade I had learned my lesson. This big kid had come up to me and before I realized what she was going to do, she pushed me roughly on the ground. I had twisted my ankle then, but that wasn't the point. The point was that the girl had bullied me and I was going

---

to do that too. When I was in 3rd grade I started making fun of kids, That's how I got my nick name "Bully Brenda". I was a good student and teacher's pet but other kids that I bullied didn't like me, but I didn't care. I heard the bell ring, so I rushed inside. The sound had made my ears ring. When I was seated inside the classroom, I saw the teacher come in. But she was holding a girls hand.

5/31

First scene:

Action:

***I ran as fast as I could down the street as the wind broke on my face and as sweat trickled down my neck like rain drops sliding off a roof.

Dialogue:

"Come on sweetie, you're going to be late if you don't hurry up" called my mom.
"Coming mom" I replied as I ate my breakfast.

Setting:

My bed felt warm as I opened my eyes and saw the familier poster of my favorite band and my night lamp on my bed post.

How I'd Summarize My Findings

Here's a summary of my takeaways from Joana's narrative writing:

Tool	Strengths	Possibilities for Growth
Narrative writing	• Focuses on a lesson/ message/theme • Attempts to build suspense, with scenes progressing logically • Uses a variety of details to develop character and plot; characters developed as archetypes ("the new girl," "the bully") • Uses a writing process, and utilizes each step of the process • Strong volume of work; writes at school and at home	• With the lesson in mind, she could draw the story out with more scenes to bring about a more realistic conclusion. • She might help make the lesson less overt. • She could use detail to show more than tell. • She might create characters who are more complex, multidimensional. • She could take risks and try things out beyond the minilesson of the day.

Excerpt from main table on pages 97–101

Making Discoveries from Informational Writing

Informational writing is an umbrella term that incorporates a variety of types of structures and subgenres, including all-about books, question-and-answer books, field guides, and reference materials. Informational writing is writing in which a writer tries to teach the reader, or inform the reader, about a topic. This writing may be research-based or based on personal expertise.

Several elements differentiate informational writing from narrative writing. Informational pieces are focused by a topic as opposed to an event or sequence of events in time. Instead of a sequence of events, informational writing is organized into sections or parts. Instead of elaborating with dialogue and setting, informational writing elaborates with factual information and added explanation on those facts. For a list of grade-level expectations for informational writing, see the CCSS Writing Standard 2.

What to Look For

Remember that as we approach an example of student writing, we are going to look at it through different lenses. These lenses, or the *qualities of good writing*, help us see more and say more about the artifact. Here, again, are the categories:

- focus
- structure
- elaboration
- conventions

I explain how I consider each category when I look at informational writing.

Focus refers to the extent to which the piece is focused on a broad or narrow topic. For example, while one student might write about animals, another might write about animals of Africa, and still another might write only about elephants. The more focused the writing, the more challenging it is to elaborate. You may also look to see how the writer is able to maintain the focus throughout the piece. For example, if a writer says she is writing about elephants but then has a chapter called "Other Animals of the African Plains," that child might be broadening her focus in order to add more detail. You can find grade-level-specific expectations in the CCSS Writing Standards 2.a and 2.e, but here are some general questions to consider and expectations to have:

Informational Writing Look-Fors: Focus

Question to Ask	Where to Look	The Ideal
Is the focus established early on in the piece? Is the focus maintained throughout?	The first section or paragraph of the piece (the introduction) as well as any chapter titles or headings throughout	The writer establishes the focus not only for the topic but also for the main idea(s) that the piece discusses.
Does the conclusion for the piece match the initial focus?	The final section or paragraph of the piece (the conclusion)	The conclusion should provide a wrap-up, reiterating the main topic as well as idea(s) in the piece.

continues

Informational Writing Look-Fors: Focus (cont.)

Question to Ask	Where to Look	The Ideal
How focused of a topic does the writer choose?	The chapter titles and headings	A narrower focus is not necessarily more ideal, although it is harder to elaborate on and develop a narrowly focused topic. What's more important is that there is a clear purpose to the piece, and that the piece is not simply a collection of everything the writer knows dumped into one document.

Structure in informational writing can be viewed on a couple of levels. There is the structure of the overall piece—introduction, subsections, and conclusion. Then there is the structure within each section—how is the information organized? Into paragraphs? With like information? Reference CCSS Writing Standards 3.a and 3.e for grade-specific information. When you look at your student's writing, consider:

Informational Writing Look-Fors: Structure

Question to Ask	Where to Look	The Ideal
Is the piece organized into paragraphs, sections, or chapters?	Scan to see if there is a table of contents listing facts, or look through the piece for the presence of paragraphs.	There is some organization with similar facts and information grouped.
Is information organized within each chapter?	Read one section/chapter to see if the facts contained relate.	When the writer declares the section or chapter to focus on a subtopic or sub–main idea, it's important that all (or most) of the facts relate back to the title.

continues

Informational Writing Look-Fors: Structure (cont.)

Question to Ask	Where to Look	The Ideal
Is each section presented in a logical way?	Recap for yourself the main subtopics that the writer is teaching about and the order in which they appear.	Information that is more fundamental or basic should come before information that is more complex.

Elaboration in an informational piece of writing should be factual. The writer may also include details that elaborate upon those facts. Facts may be from personal expertise, quotations from other sources, or summarized information from other sources. Writers may elaborate on those facts by including more explanation, a definition of key terms, or an analogy. It is also important to consider how precise a writer's word choice is. When writing about a topic, it is important to use the vocabulary that an expert about that topic would use. For example, when writing about clouds, a writer should use words like *cumulus* and *stratus*, not just *white* and *fluffy*. For grade-level-specific expectations, see CCSS 2.b and 2.d.

Informational Writing Look-Fors: Elaboration

Question to Ask	Where to Look	The Ideal
What types of information does the writer include?	Across the piece, look to see the types of information—both facts and details to elaborate on the facts.	The writer uses a variety in the types of detail—facts from her own knowledge, definitions of terms, information from outside sources. The writer considers the audience and adds details that help teach about the topic.
How concrete are the details the writer includes?	When the writer is writing about a topic or concept, notice whether the details feel vague or specific.	The writer should use precise language, appropriate to the audience.
How precise is the vocabulary the writer uses?	Notice whether the author uses content-specific vocabulary (vocabulary that relates to the topic being discussed).	Vocabulary is appropriate to the topic and is explained or defined when the audience is assumed to not come to the text already knowing the terms.

In looking at the student piece with the lens of *conventions*, consider the same set of questions laid out in the "Narrative Writing" section.

A Sample Analysis: Joana

Joana has no published informational writing from within months of the assessment window (May) from which all the other data come. There is a minimal amount of prewriting in her notebook—really just a list of facts about a topic.

I can extrapolate from her notebook, however, that she seems to feel most comfortable with narrative writing and poetry. Whenever given choice of what kind of writing she'd like to do at home, she tends to choose stories and poems. Therefore, informational writing may be one type of writing that she could take a risk to try out.

How I'd Summarize My Findings

Since Joana doesn't have a completed piece of informational writing to analyze, I'd summarize my findings like this:

Tool	Strengths	Next Steps
Informational writing	N/A	• She could take risks and try to explore topics of interest to write about.

Excerpt from main table on pages 97–101

Making Discoveries from Opinion Writing

Opinion writing is also an umbrella term that includes many types of writing. Children in younger grades may first try their hand at opinion writing by crafting letters that try to persuade someone of something (such as a letter to the school principal to change the lunch menu) or a review of something (the student's favorite video game). Older writers may write thesis-driven types of writing such as essays or speeches.

Although the structures of these different types of writing may vary slightly, what they all have in common is that the author has a clear viewpoint, or opinion, and is setting about trying to convince the reading audience of that opinion. Often, the writer supports his opinion with reasons and information in an attempt to persuade his audience.

The CCSS Writing Standard 1 relates to opinion writing; refer to that document for grade-specific expectations.

What to Look For

As with the other two main categories of writing (narrative and informational writing), the qualities of good writing are helpful to use when examining opinion writing. Again, those categories are:

- focus
- structure
- elaboration
- conventions

When a writer attempts to *focus* an opinion piece of writing, the writing will be focused on that writer's opinion. The age and sophistication of the writer depend on the sophistication of the idea. The "opinion" focus for an older writer might also be called a "thesis statement." When looking at an opinion piece of writing, consider the CCSS Writing 1.a and 1.d, as well as these questions:

Opinion Writing Look-Fors: Focus

Question to Ask	Where to Look	The Ideal
Is the piece organized into paragraphs, sections, or chapters?	The first and/or last paragraphs	Typically, a writer states the claim or thesis statement within the first paragraph and may reiterate it in the final paragraph.
Does the writer maintain support for his opinion throughout the piece?	Each body paragraph's topic sentence and details within the body paragraphs	The writer should support the main thesis statement with reasons (topic sentences of body paragraphs) and examples (details within each body paragraph).
Does the writer offer opposing information? If so, how is it used?	Throughout the piece	The writer should be able use opposing information to elucidate the main point, not to seem wishy-washy and unable to "take a side."

The *structure* of an opinion piece may, at first blush, look something like an informational piece. Ideally there is some sort of introducing statement or section, a body, and a concluding statement or section. The actual structure may vary somewhat by type of opinion writing. For example, a book review is slightly different in organization than a persuasive essay or a speech. You can ask yourself the same questions about structure for informational and opinion writing. See CCSS 1.a and 1.d for more grade-specific expectation. Consider, as you read the piece:

Opinion Writing Look-Fors: Structure

Question to Ask	Where to Look	The Ideal
Is the piece organized into paragraphs, sections, or chapters?	Look through the piece for the presence of paragraphs.	There is some organization with similar facts and information grouped.
Is information organized within each paragraph?	Read one section/chapter to see if the information contained relates to the topic sentence.	When the writer declares the paragraph to focus on a reason, it's important that all (or most) of the facts relate back to that reason.
Is each paragraph presented in a logical order?	Recap for yourself the main reasons the writer offers as supports for his opinion. Consider whether they seem of equal importance or if some should come before others.	It is often more readable when information that is more fundamental should come before information that is more complex.

The *elaboration* of an opinion piece likely includes opinions, reasons, and examples. For older writers, reasons can be considered the categories within the overarching opinion, and the examples can be considered support for the reasons. For example, if the writer is trying to persuade the audience that New York City is the best city, then reasons might be categories, such as best parks, best buildings, and best restaurants. Examples would then support those reasons. Under "best parks," we might learn about Central Park, Gramercy Park, and Washington Square Park. Consider CCSS Writing Standard 1.b and the following guiding questions:

Opinion Writing Look-Fors: Elaboration

Question to Ask	Where to Look	The Ideal
Are there examples to support the reasons?	Within each body paragraph	The writer should support each reason with several facts and details. Facts and details should be varied and specific.
How convincing are the reasons and examples?	Within each body paragraph	The reasons and examples should be clear, strong, and convincing.
Does the writer seem to consider her audience when choosing reasons and examples?	Within each body paragraph	The writer shouldn't repeat information that is obvious to the intended audience, but instead use information that helps convince the reader of her point.

Refer again to the previous section "Narrative Writing" and the CCSS Language Standards as you consider the strength of the student's control of *conventions*.

A Sample Analysis: Joana

In Figure 2.21, you can see that Joana has done some work in her writer's notebook toward opinion writing. She seems to have collected entries to write both personal essays as well as literary essays.

From this work, it's clear that a strength for Joana is making a claim and supporting her claim with reasons: in the T-chart entry (undated), she has six reasons to support the claim that "It is important that we save animals that are about to be extinct." She also has planned to include some personal anecdotes to support her claim in an earlier entry on October 29.

This work is from early in fourth grade, and I'm reluctant to draw conclusions about how it relates to the work she is currently doing as a writer at the end of fourth grade.

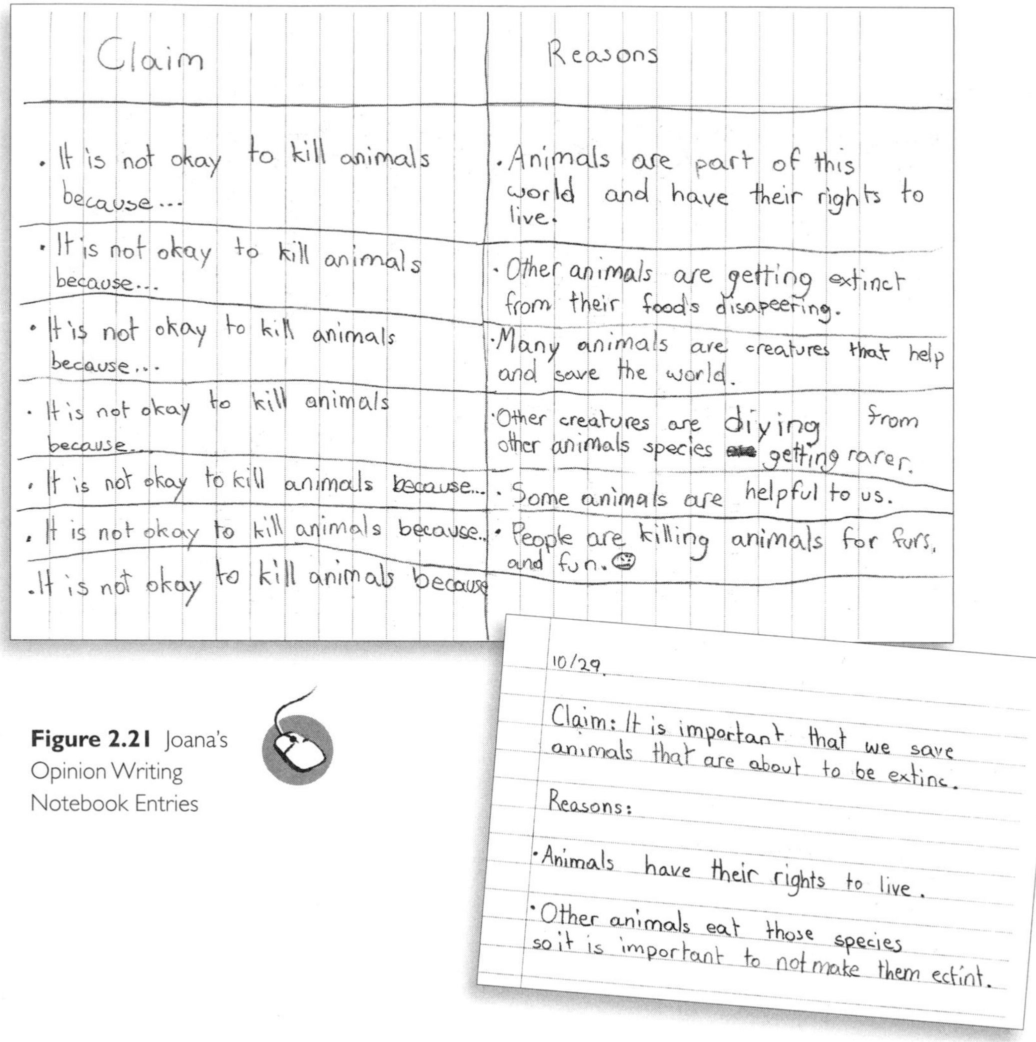

Claim	Reasons
• It is not okay to kill animals because...	• Animals are part of this world and have their rights to live.
• It is not okay to kill animals because...	• Other animals are getting extinct from their food's disapeering.
• It is not okay to kill animals because...	• Many animals are creatures that help and save the world.
• It is not okay to kill animals because...	• Other creatures are diying from other animals species are getting rarer.
• It is not okay to kill animals because...	• Some animals are helpful to us.
• It is not okay to kill animals because...	• People are killing animals for furs, and fun. ☺
• It is not okay to kill animals because...	

Figure 2.21 Joana's Opinion Writing Notebook Entries

10/29

Claim: It is important that we save animals that are about to be extinc.

Reasons:

• Animals have their rights to live.

• Other animals eat those species so it is important to not make them ectint.

How I'd Summarize My Findings

Tool	Strengths	Next Steps
Opinion writing	• Makes a claim • Supports claim with reasons • Has a strategy for elaboration (personal anecdotes)	• There is no current work from which to draw possible next steps.

Excerpt from main table on pages 97–101

ACTION ➡

Now's the time to take a look at your student's writing or Alex's narrative. Remember that you can see my thinking about Alex's work in Appendix A, and you can use it to compare against your own interpretations.

☐ Wrap-Up

Phew. You made it. If you've made your way through this chapter, working to understand Joana as well as another student, you've probably spent a good deal of time. You might be wondering, "How am I going to do this with all thirty of my students?" You don't necessarily have to. This process might be most helpful in crafting meaningful goals for your Response to Intervention–identified student. Or maybe you decide to go through the process for each student once a year. I have a few pieces of good news for you.

First, it'll get easier. Not right away, but the more you go through this process, you'll find that things just jump off the page at you where before you had to study and study to figure out a student's strengths and needs.

Second, you hopefully learned a lot of content by working through this process with just one student's work so far. You learned what questions to ask of the data and what it looks like when a student's work shows strong understanding. Hopefully you also identified gaps in your *own* content knowledge. You may look back at Chapter 1 for some suggested professional reading to help with that goal.

Third, this work is going to pay off big time. By looking this closely at your student's work, you're going to be choosing teaching that is going to make a big difference and will help you see dramatic progress.

ACTION ➡

Reflect to set professional goal(s) for yourself. Think about which pieces of student work you found most difficult to analyze. What are the areas of reading or writing that those examples of student work align with? Collect some resources (see Chapter 1) to help you.

☐ What's Next?

In the next chapter, I'm going to walk you through the next step of the process: synthesizing the data and setting a goal. It's here that we take what we noticed about each individual piece of data, put it together, and notice patterns and trends. Make sure you have your one complete table with strengths and needs ready to go.

Chapter 3

Interpreting Data and Establishing a Goal

> Set goals—high goals . . .
> When [you have] a goal
> to shoot for, you create
> teamwork, people working
> for a common good.
> —**Paul William
> "Bear" Bryant**

Evelyn was a mystery. Chatty, lively, with a perpetually bouncing ponytail, she was one of the stronger readers in my third-grade class— and she puzzled me.

She shared deep and thoughtful ideas during read-aloud. Her writing work was filled with voice and detail. But without fail, during reading workshop I looked over to find her curled up with Poppleton, a book far below her independent reading level. She was engaged, sure. She kept her log up perfectly and read for the required time and then some. But I couldn't figure out how to get her to stick with chapter books I knew would challenge her thinking.

Of course my first step was to ask Evelyn herself what was up. I thought that perhaps she was just coasting on the ease and familiarity of Poppleton. Evelyn was not forthcoming—"I just like them, that's all," she said, and clammed up. Stumped, I decided to spend some more time Evelyn-watching—and collecting data about what I saw. The next day, engagement inventory in hand, I watched as Evelyn went over to the class library to choose a book. She picked up a couple of chapter books. I expected her to turn them over to read the blurb, or to study the cover, or to read the first few pages. She did none of those things. She opened the first book, swept her fingers across the pages, and set it down. She did the same with the next book. I watched her do this a couple more times before snagging a well-thumbed Poppleton book from the basket and going to sit down. I wrote down what I saw.

It was a few minutes later that the lightbulb went off: The chapter books that I'd ordered for 99¢ through the book club catalogue had rough pulp paper pages. She didn't like the feel on her hands, and she preferred the smoothness of the Poppleton pages. It wasn't about content or book level or engagement or her state of mind—it was about sensation!

Later, in a conference with Evelyn, I was able to bring up what I noticed. She and I started to brainstorm some solutions so that she could be comfortable reading the sorts of books that would help her grow as a reader.

If I had relied on my assumptions rather than what I saw and recorded in the engagement inventory, I might have completely missed the mark with Evelyn. When interpretations of students' reading needs are not based on data—or not based on *helpful* data—they are often based on what *the interpreter* wants to see. All of us bring our own experiences and mind-sets to bear when we are thinking about students—how can we not?

If I had asked Evelyn's reading partner what she thought about Evelyn reading Poppleton, she might have assumed it was because of the pictures. The teacher down the hall may have concluded that she was just not up for a challenge. Her mother might have nostalgically assumed that Evelyn was just enjoying books she'd loved since she was little. But the data reveal truths about our students as readers and writers that we might miss otherwise. Our job is to interpret that data and use it to set goals for our students that will make a real difference in their reading lives.

In this chapter, I lead you through the process of making interpretations about the student work you analyzed during the previous chapter—student work that offers the kind of information you can use to make sound teaching decisions.

Upon arriving at this chapter, the most time-consuming part of this process is behind you: analyzing all the data separately to name what they say about a student's strengths and needs. If you have been following along using your own student's work (or the samples from Alex included in Appendix A), you now have a complete table listing out many possible avenues for instruction. Here's where we are in the process:

- Step 1: Collect data.
- Step 2: Analyze data.
X - **Step 3: Interpret data and establish a goal.**
- Step 4: Create an action plan.

Marvel at all you've discovered about Alex, or the student whose work you've chosen to study. Some of it you may have already known. Some of it may be new. Some of it may even contradict what you *thought* you knew.

This discovery contradicting prior knowledge used to happen all the time when I was a teacher, and it happens all of the time when I'm leading teachers through this protocol. A teacher brings a stack of work and begins with a disclaimer or preface about the student. Recently, a third-grade teacher brought the work of a child she was concerned about because he seemed stuck in superficial-level comprehension and thinking when he read and wrote. His narratives lacked insight and his reading work was mostly retelling. By going through this process, however, we discovered that the best thing we could do was actually help him with strategies for staying focused and engaged in his work—once we went down that path, he became much more interpretive!

Many of us can relate to this. Sometimes a dominant trait of a reader/writer in your classroom jumps out and demands your attention. For many of us, this might be a child's tendency to write with hard to read spelling. Or maybe it's a child's fidgetiness during independent work time.

What's fascinating to me is that following the four-step protocol will often illuminate one of our own habitual missteps in trying to teach in a data-based way. Sometimes, it's our tendency as teachers to focus heavily on the most salient observations, falsely assuming that because it's the most obvious, it's also the most important. Or perhaps you realize that the work you've been collecting and using to form goals all along really didn't provide the depth you thought it did. Or perhaps you find that you were sometimes making excuses for students, explaining away their lack of progress with something that really was unrelated to the work they were doing in the classroom.

ACTION →

Think of a few children in your class whose data you plan to look at by using this protocol. Jot a quick list of what you think might be the most important thing to work on for each of them. Save the list and compare it to what you discover and decide to be the most important after using the protocol to study their work.

Missteps aside, this chapter will help you take all the information, all the possibilities you've arrived at thus far through analysis of the data, and make a decision about what to teach. We'll sort through all the possible areas for growth to arrive at a clear goal—one that spans both reading and writing. One that will focus the differentiated instruction for weeks or maybe even months to come. One that will make the biggest difference for each student in your class.

◻ Why Is Goal Setting Important?

Think for a moment about the last time you were proud of an accomplishment. When you set out to accomplish what you did, do you remember stating a goal at the outset? "I want to run that marathon" or "This year I'm going to commit to eating out less and cooking at home more" or "This weekend we're going to organize that garage so I can fit my car inside." Goals affect accomplishment—when we have a clear sense of what we want to accomplish, how we will attempt to accomplish it, and our deadline for accomplishing it, we are more likely to be motivated to succeed (Pink 2011).

Reading and writing are no different. Stated goals hold students and their teachers accountable. When goals come from an accurate assessment of what's really going on with a reader, when they are decided upon in conversation with the student and supported over time, readers accomplish more and succeed more.

Hattie (1999) and Petty (2006) have shown in their research that "achievement is enhanced to the degree that students and teachers set and communicate appropriate, specific, and challenging goals" (Petty, 63). Fisher, Frey, and Lapp (2012) agree: "Goal setting should be a regular part of the instructional design process" (81). You are now ready to begin setting that appropriate, specific, and challenging goal with your student and to begin helping the student toward increased achievement. Ideally, you decide on a goal using the data you've collected, and then, in conversation with the student, you help her to recognize and understand what you've discovered.

Once a goal is established, you teach and provide feedback to the student over time about his progress toward that goal. Feedback is shown to have a major influence on performance (Hattie 1999). Ericsson, Krampe, and Tesch-Römer (1993) note that motivation does not always come from enjoyment of the task (although of course we want children to enjoy reading and writing!) but rather from recognizing that hours of practice yield increased performance. They advocate "repeated experiences in which the individual can attend to the critical aspects of the situation and incrementally improve her or his performance in response to knowledge of results, feedback, or both from a teacher" (398).

So, of the long list you've created of possible areas for growth, which one do you pick? To help my decision making, I tend to do two things: I look for patterns, and then I apply the 80/20 principle, which I explain in detail later in this chapter.

Looking for Patterns: Triangulating the Data

To choose a goal that is going to have the biggest possible effect on a student's progress, it's got to be something important. The goal needs to be something for which you see instructional opportunity in both reading and writing, so that when you and the student are working on the goal, you have opportunities across the day to practice. Seeing the same teaching opportunity when looking at more than one work artifact also tells you that the need wasn't a fluke—it wasn't a result of the assignment or task, and it wasn't a result of the student missing breakfast one day or being distracted by an argument with her mom that morning.

When I look at the long list of options, I often try to triangulate—or at least *bi*angulate— the data. I try to see where a potential area of growth crops up in more than one place, examining more than one artifact, in both reading and in writing. Sometimes, in working toward this kind of synthesis, I may realize that I didn't state a similar goal in the exact same way in each artifact, but if I can adjust and restate, more than one possible goal will fit together.

Let's look together at the table we've created by studying Joana's work (Figure 3.1).

Tool	Strengths	Possibilities for Growth
Engagement inventory	• Has strategies to get started reading • Can sustain reading for long periods of time • Jots about her reading to hold onto ideas	• Is she switching to a new book in the midst of another chapter book? If so, perhaps work to sustain focus on one book the entire time.

Figure 3.1 Table Created from Studying and Analyzing Joana's Work   *continues*

Tool	Strengths	Possibilities for Growth
Book log	• Chooses books that are a good fit, and in a variety of genres • Reads at an appropriate page-per-minute rate • Reads for about sixty minutes/day. • Reads at home and at school • Reads an appropriate level	• She could learn to read until she's done reading, perhaps stopping at a place that's good for the book, not when the timer goes off. • She could work on reading one book until completion before starting another.
Reading interest survey	• Reflects on her love of reading and in the fantasy genre specifically	• She could connect outside-of-reading interests to reading to help expand her book choices.
Writing about reading	• Makes interpretations • Uses social issues as a way to make interpretations • Empathizes with characters • Uses words to describe characters • Provides some text evidence	• She could develop interpretations that are less obvious. • She could see characters in a more complex way. • She could analyze secondary characters. • She could use more precise language when analyzing characters. • She might apply the same level of analysis to nonfiction books. • She could provide more detailed text evidence.

Tool	Strengths	Possibilities for Growth
Whole-book assessment (using *Independent Reading Assessment: Fiction* [Serravallo 2012])	• Can name the time and place • Connects significant events • Names multiple traits about main character, showing complexity • Understands meaning of unknown words and phrases, and uses context to explain • Interprets theme, social issues, and symbolism	• She could add original details when describing time and place. • She could connect several significant events. • She could name multiple traits about secondary characters to show complexity.
Fluency (from running record)	• Appropriate phrasing • Matches the intonation to the meaning in the text • Automaticity • Attends to punctuation	N/A
Running record	• Successfully uses all three cueing systems • Reads accurately and automatically • Retells correctly, briefly • Answers comprehension questions correctly, briefly • Understands words used figuratively	• She could elaborate during retell and when answering comprehension questions.

continues

Tool	Strengths	Possibilities for Growth
Conversation transcript	• Polite and patient, follows agreed-upon rules for discussion • Listens carefully to sort through and synthesize others' ideas • Supports ideas with text evidence • Interprets theme • Takes into account multiple plots and characters	• She could advocate for herself more in conversation to allow her ideas to be heard.
Narrative writing	• Focuses on a lesson/message/theme • Attempts to build suspense, with scenes progressing logically • Uses a variety of details to develop character and plot; characters developed as archetypes ("the new girl," "the bully") • Uses a writing process, and utilizes each step of the process • Strong volume of work; writes at school and at home	• With the lesson in mind, she could draw the story out with more scenes to bring about a more realistic conclusion. • She might help make the lesson less overt. • She could use detail to show more than tell. • She might create characters who are more complex, multidimensional. • She could take risks and try things out beyond the minilesson of the day.
Informational writing	N/A	• She could take risks and try to explore topics of interest to write about.

Tool	Strengths	Possibilities for Growth
Opinion writing	• Makes a claim • Supports claim with reasons • Has a strategy for elaboration (personal anecdotes)	• There is no current work from which to draw possible next steps.

As I look at this chart during this phase of the protocol, I'm going to focus on the third (right) column. I can focus my attention only on that column because I am confident that when doing my initial analysis, I made sure that every possible area of growth comes from a strength. I'm aiming to state a possible goal and to back up my decision with evidence from my analysis of Joana's work with more than one data tool. I use a general language frame—a sort of template—to force me to seek out patterns as I craft a goal for Joana, so that an idea of lesser importance doesn't just jump off the page and demand my attention. Notice that I list reading and writing goals that are related, and offer support from my findings in column three of the summary chart:

I think [student] could learn [possible goal in reading] and [related possible goal in writing] because in reading, I noticed [findings from column #3] and in writing I noticed [findings from column #3].

In this step of the protocol, I also try to be sure to push myself to name several possible goals. My thinking about this is similar to my thinking around the need to triangulate. I want to make sure that I'm not just grasping at any isolated idea that jumps off the page. In doing this work with hundreds of teachers, I've found that it's often the case that the first thing you see as a teacher is the thing you want to see—the thing you expect to see. Or sometimes, it's the thing that is your thing as a teacher. Some of us tend to fixate on grammar, others are big on the importance of details and description, others care most about deep interpretive reading. By listing out several possibilities, you force yourself to think beyond your first gut instinct, and you may end up landing on an option that is more important for a reader. I try to articulate four or five goals at this stage.

For Joana, here are five possible goals and the evidence for why I think these goals might matter for her:

ACTION →

After studying the possible goals for Joanna, take out the summary table of your ideas about Alex. Try this same work of naming several possible goals and backing up your thinking by providing evidence across pieces of data. When possible, look across reading and writing. Jot your thoughts down first, and then take a look in Appendix A to see my thinking.

Possible goal #1: I think Joana could learn to come up with more original interpretations when she reads and creates stories that have less obvious lessons/themes when she writes because she is a student who is already attuned to theme in both her reading and writing. In her reading, she tends to think first about the obvious themes. In her writing, she makes theme very obvious to her reader.

Possible goal #2: I think Joana could learn to do more character development in her writing, and character analysis in her reading (especially secondary characters) because she is able to come up with basic traits in her reading and spends some time developing characters as she creates stories. However, the characters in her fiction story tend to be two-dimensional, almost stereotypes/archetypes constructed to help convey her message. In her reading, she tends to see her characters as one way rather than as multidimensional.

Possible goal #3: I think Joana could learn to take more risks, owning her process as a reader, writer, and conversationalist more. She seems to be a good student—trying out her teacher's lesson of the day whether in reading or writing. She could learn to reflect more on the processes and strategies that push her the most as a learner and/or to even invent some of her own strategies to explore reading and writing.

Possible goal #4: I think Joana could learn to develop her work with more detail in both reading and writing. As a reader, Joana tends to back up her ideas with a small, simple detail from the text (from "Writing about

*reading") and could elaborate with more detail ("Independent reading
assessment"). As a writer, Joana could work on details that show, not tell.*

*Possible goal #5: I think Joana could try to balance out her reading and
writing life by including more informational texts. In her reading notebook, all
she writes about is fiction, although she does read nonfiction as evidenced by
her reading log. In her writing notebook, she only begins with some informational topic ideas, but never brings them through the process.*

To finalize the goal-setting process, I either choose one of them to begin working on
with Joana or decide to further synthesize, putting a couple of related goals together.
When choosing a goal, I use the 80/20 principle.

Applying the 80/20 Principle: Choosing a Goal

The 80/20 principle, also known as the *Pareto principle* or the *Pareto rule*, refers to the
idea that 20 percent of something has the potential to cause or create 80 percent of the
result. To put it another way, a minority of input can yield a majority of output. Pareto
first made this observation in Italy in relation to economics. Pareto noticed that 80
percent of Italy's land was owned by 20 percent of the population. He then carried out
surveys on a variety of other countries and found to his surprise that a similar distribu-
tion applied (Koch 2008, Gladwell 2002).

This statistical finding has implications for your personal life (20 percent of what you
do accounts for 80 percent of your happiness), for business (80 percent of revenue comes
from 20 percent of initiatives), and even in the teaching of reading and writing. In reading
and writing, I'd like to assert that one goal of the four or five I articulated will make 80
percent of the difference in Joana's reading and writing life.

In essence, I try to work smarter, not harder. I try to find the 20 percent thing that
makes the 80 percent difference. I try to focus my energies and efforts, and I help the
student to do so as well.

Looking across all of the possibilities for what would help the student, what one thing
will make the biggest difference? What 20 percent of her reading needs, when worked
on consistently over the next month or so, will yield an 80 percent improvement? Which
goals might impact other goals? For example, paying more attention to characters (#2)
might help her make better interpretations (#1). Or asking her to be more detailed (#4)

might help her to see more in her characters (#2).

I want to choose a goal that I think has the potential to impact the others. For example, I think that deeper character analysis can ripple into interpretation. Sometimes secondary characters are often sage, wise characters who

ACTION ⟶

Apply the 80/20 principle to Alex's goals or the goals of the student you're investigating. Articulate your final decision about the student's goal. To see my thinking about Alex's work, turn to Appendix A.

offer advice and counsel to the main character, and if I can get Joana to study them more closely, it might help her to understand less salient themes. It's also possible that looking more closely at characters will help her be more detailed in her writing and responses to reading. If she can see the characters in the books she reads as more well-rounded, she'll have more to say in her responses. If she develops her characters more completely and brings that development into her drafts, then she'll write about the characters with more detail. Therefore, for Joana, I choose to go with #2—working more with characters.

The First Teaching Opportunity: The Goal-Setting Conference

Now that you have articulated a goal for your student, it's time to bring the student in to a goal-setting conference. In my mind, the goal-setting conference is the first conference occurring after the teacher has chosen a goal to work toward. After this conference, with the support of the next chapter, you will plan strategies and methods for ongoing instruction—but first, it's important to get the student on board.

It's well established that the more a person takes ownership of her own goal, the more likely it is that the goal will be accomplished (see, for example, Pink 2011). The more we lead students toward the articulation of their own goals, the more investment they have in working to accomplish that goal.

I say "lead students" because without your leadership, it's likely that the student would choose a more superficial, obvious, or basic goal. Ask a student to articulate a goal without any guidance, and the student usually says something like "I want to read every night for thirty minutes" or "I want to read faster" or "I'm going to try to write longer stories." This "longer, faster, more" is generally what students believe makes for a better reader or writer.

On the other hand, participating in a goal-setting conference that is grounded in some of the student's own data, during which conversation is guided by your careful questioning, can help a student realize things about his work or process or skill level that he may not have otherwise considered.

Now, you haven't spent all of this time analyzing the student's work for the student to choose some goal from out in left-field. You need to be prepared to steer the conversation toward helping the student realize for himself what you've realized in his absence. So it takes some degree of skill on your part to help lead the child to notice what you noticed.

Be sure to gather only the work from your stack that would help a child notice what you noticed. For example, if you want the student to notice her tendency toward being distracted, you might choose to have the child's reading log (which would show a problematic page-per-minute rate) and writing notebook (which would show overly short entries). Alternatively, if you want a student to realize that his work tends to be literal, you might choose to gather a few examples of the student's writing about reading that shows retelling and some other student's work that shows more inferential thinking. For Joana, I'm going to present the independent reading assessment, some of her writing about reading from her Book Lover's Book (her reading notebook), and her fiction story. See Figure 3.2 for more ideas.

Gathering Materials for the Goal-Setting Conference

Sample Goal	Materials to Use During the Goal-Setting Conference
Work on inference when reading fiction and on show, not tell when writing narratives.	Sticky notes that show literal responses to reading, a mostly summarized narrative without much description or elaboration, and/or a running record with inferential questions marked as incorrect
Work on main idea and supporting details. In reading, be able to summarize key information from the text. In writing, use topic sentences and relevant details to elaborate.	A sample of informational writing with lists of facts not organized with topic sentences, sticky notes showing the student recording random facts from the reading, and/or a written summary of a book read that has many facts without main idea statements
Work on focus and attention during reading and writing workshops.	Reading logs showing a slower-than-ideal reading rate, writing notebook entries that are short and/or unfinished, and/or an engagement inventory showing distracted behavior

Figure 3.2

Once you've gathered those materials that will help the student realize the same potential area of growth that you did, you can set aside about five to ten minutes to have a conversation with the student. I usually begin by stating my intention for our time together: that we're going to look over some of the student's work together and decide on one ambitious goal that will make the biggest difference in his reading and writing for the next month or two. I state the intention in that way so that the goal setting becomes bigger than "I want to read every night for thirty minutes." Through my questioning and guidance, the goal will not only be ambitious but also specific.

Next, I lay the work on the table in front of us and ask the student to look with me. I ask the student what she notices about the work. This inquiry can often benefit from careful, leading questions (see sidebar). Many students also benefit from seeing a contrastive example— another student's work, a rubric, or a sample of work from a prior lesson— in order to be able to articulate how their work could be improved.

After a few minutes of conversation with the student where you question and prompt his thinking, you establish a clear goal together. Chances are good that the student will need you to articulate the goal clearly. You might say something like, "So it sounds like a good goal for you would be to ____ in reading and ____ in writing."

As soon as the goal is clear, many find it helpful for the teacher or student to jot that goal on a sticky note, goal card, bookmark, or some other form to make it official (see Figure 3.4, page 112 for one example). This tangible reminder of the goal will also be a way for the

> ## Some Questions and Prompts to Use During Goal-Setting Conferences
>
> - What can you notice about your work?
> - How does your work compare to [provide work of another student, an author, or exemplar]?
> - Can you think of any ways that you might improve your work?
> - Let's talk about some of the things you think you're good at as a reader or writer.
> - What do you think might be a good goal for you based on what we've noticed?
> - When you look at your work, what are some things you seem to struggle with?
> - Is there anything you notice from this (rubric, other student's work, etc.) that you think you'd like to try to start doing?
> - What's going to make the biggest difference for you as a reader/writer?
> - What is some new work you think you're ready to start taking on?
> - One thing I notice is _____. What are your thoughts about that?

student, her parents, and any other service providers to stay focused and clear on the work ahead.

Next, help the student to begin on his journey toward accomplishing the goal with one clear strategy for either reading or writing that he can start right away. Make it clear that this is the first of many strategies you'll introduce during the upcoming weeks.

As with any guided practice structure, it's helpful to not only mention the strategy but also to give the student a quick chance to try the work in front of you as you offer support. Don't fret if the student has yet to achieve perfection with the strategy—if he did, you might worry that your goal wasn't ambitious enough! Instead, make notes to yourself about the level of support the student needed as you practiced the strategy together.

End the conference by repeating the goal and the first strategy you offered to the student to begin work on the goal. Let the student know when you'll next see her and what you expect to happen between now and then. For example, are you expecting the student to write anything down to show she's been practicing what you just taught? Do you want the student to be ready to show you anything a few days from now? Based on how this student learns, you may choose to write this plan down as well.

Read the goal-setting conference that follows. I've included conferring tips embedded within the transcript to help elucidate some of the moves within the conference that are applicable to any conference. More about the structure of conferences can be found in Chapter 4. As you read this conference, notice that I'm employing an inquiry approach. Notice my questioning techniques to try to support Joana in noticing what I've noticed about her work.

Goal-Setting Conference with Joana

T: Hi, Joana. I've been spending some time looking at some of your work and I thought we could meet to talk about how your reading and writing have been going and to set some goals for the work you might do over the coming month or two. I've chosen a couple of things we could look at together. Here I have some of your recent Book Lover's Book entries, and here's the story you just published. I also grabbed the independent reading assessment you took where you read *Sadako and the Thousand Paper Cranes*.

[I spread the work out on the table in front of us.]

J: *[nods]*

T: OK, so what we want to do here is to look at these three pieces of work and see if together we can find something you're strong at, but that you want to get even better at. Take a minute to look it over and tell me what you're thinking.

[Starting with strengths helps keep the tone of the conference positive and encouraging.]

J: I think that in all three I'm really thinking a lot about the theme.

T: I agree. You clearly thought about bullying when you wrote your story. And when you write about your reading, you are writing to try to come up with theme. What else?

J: I come up with character traits a lot when I am reading. And I like to come up with my own characters and write stories about them.

T: I agree with that, too. Like, here, when you read Sadako, you wrote that she's determined and confident. And in your fiction story, you really tried to think about creating two characters who were very different and who changed across the story. Anything else?

[Notice how I'm trying to leave the questioning open-ended, like an inquiry. I want to support the student's noticing of her own work. When she says something seemingly simple or basic, I try to make a bigger deal of it, explicitly naming and elaborating on her strengths.]

J: I really like reading and I like writing and I think I'm understanding a lot of what I read when I read.

T: I'm so happy to hear that because your work really does show that. I can see from how much you put into your writing and into your Book Lover's Book that you really enjoy stories. You think about characters in your books and develop them in your writing like you said, and you think about what the story is really about—the lessons and messages to take away. Let's think now about a goal. How do you think you can grow?

[This next part of the conference takes a bit more guidance. If Joana already knew what she had to do grow, she might just well do it! Often the teacher at this point needs to provide ideas or examples of other work that help give students an image of what to strive for.]

J: I'm not sure. Maybe give more details about my characters?

T: What do you mean by that?

J: Like, give examples for why I'm thinking what I'm thinking.

T: Well, do you think that's going to help you grow?

J: I'm not sure.

T: Well, I agree with you that maybe there is more you can do with your characters. Let me show you some examples of how some other students talked about Sadako, and her family, and see if you can tell me what you see that might be something to strive for.

[Here, I'm providing her with an example so that she can look for possible ways to grow. I'm going to show her the exceptional responses—the highest category—from the independent reading assessment.]

J: Well, it seems like this person wrote a lot of different ideas about the characters, not just one idea. It's like he tried to see a couple different sides.

T: I think that's really perceptive, Joana. What are your thoughts about that?

J: Well I guess if I tried to see my character in a couple different ways then I'd have more perspectives.

T: Let's see if this goal of yours would fit with your writing too.

J: Well I already have characters in my book. And in my writer's notebook I thought about their traits.

T: Right. Do you think you're looking at the character you created in one way or many ways? And how about the other characters besides the main character?

J: Well one of my characters is really the bully and one is the victim. And then the bully learns a lesson so she changes.

T: I agree. We see a different side of Jenny by the end of the story. Let's look at where you developed your characters in your writer's notebook.

[I open up to where Joana writes about her characters in her notebook, Figure 3.3]

J: I guess Jenny is kind of all bad and Janie is all good.

T: So what do you think about this as being a goal to work on in reading and writing? Thinking about doing some deeper work with characters, trying to see how they are complex in the stories you read, and trying to create characters that are more complex in the stories you write.

[I've now articulated the goal for her. The next step is to get her started with a strategy.]

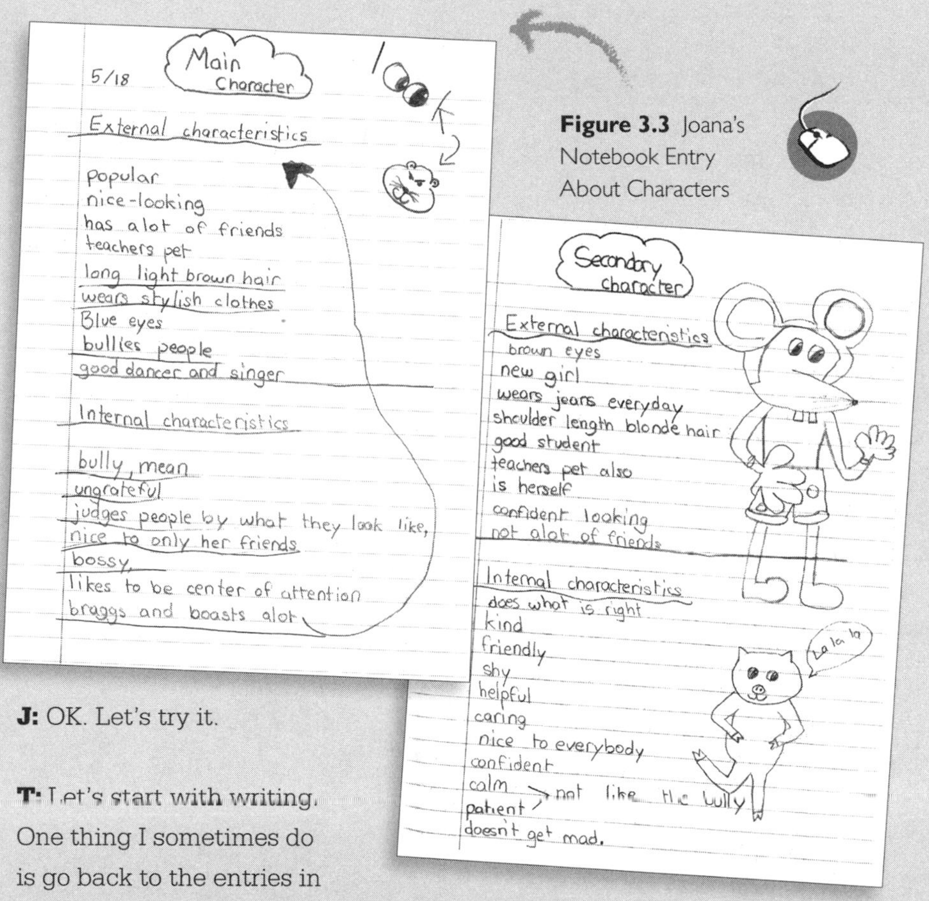

5/18
Main Character
look
External characteristics
popular
nice-looking
has alot of friends
teachers pet
long light brown hair
wears stylish clothes
Blue eyes
bullies people
good dancer and singer
Internal characteristics
bully, mean
ungrateful
judges people by what they look like,
nice to only her friends
bossy,
likes to be center of attention
braggs and boasts alot

Secondary character
External characteristics
brown eyes
new girl
wears jeans everyday
shoulder length blonde hair
good student
teachers pet also
is herself
confident looking
not alot of friends
Internal characteristics
does what is right
kind
friendly
shy
helpful
caring
nice to everybody
confident
calm
patient
not like the bully
doesn't get mad.
La la la

Figure 3.3 Joana's Notebook Entry About Characters

J: OK. Let's try it.

T: Let's start with writing. One thing I sometimes do is go back to the entries in my notebook where I've developed my character. I think about the kinds of things that *support* my character—what helps him or her overcome challenges? And then I think about things that *harm* my character—what makes the challenges harder to overcome?

J: If I had to think about Jenny, I'd say that the thing that kind of helps a little is that she has a mom who is really nice, and she notices how kind she is, and I think that helps her to make a change.

[A large part of this conference is about leading the child through self-reflection. Although I do introduce a strategy, I don't spend an enormous

amount of time working with her on it. This is the start of a goal that will focus her work in reading and writing for weeks to come. This is only the first meeting we'll have together.]

T: I think that's a good start at thinking about your character in more complex ways. I'm going to leave you with a few things that you can use during reading and writing. First, I'm going to write down the goal that we talked about on a sticky note [Figure 3.4]. You can keep this on your desk to remind and focus you. Second, I'm going to leave you with this list of character traits [Figure 3.5]. Notice the list is divided into traits that tend to be more positive and those that tend to be more negative. This might help to get you thinking about the characters in your books and those you are creating during writing.

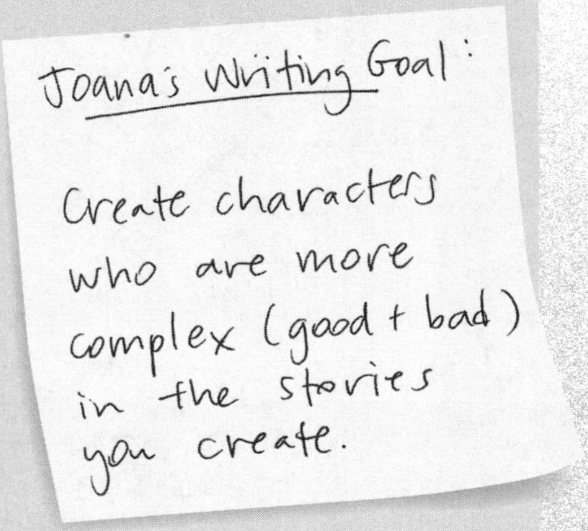

Joana's Writing Goal:

Create characters who are more complex (good + bad) in the stories you create.

Figure 3.4 Joana's Goal on a Sticky Note

J: OK, sounds good.

T: So I'll see you again in a couple of days and I'll spend more time helping you practice the strategy. In the meantime, anytime you're thinking about your character in more complex ways—either during reading or writing—I'd like you to jot down your thinking so I can see what you've been up to.

J: Where, in my notebook?

T: Probably in your writing notebook during writing workshop, and in your reading notebook or on sticky notes during reading workshop.

Traits that often help characters to overcome obstacles	Traits that often harm characters or make their problems worse
Ambitious	Angry
Brave	Annoyed
Bright	Arrogant
Careful	Bossy
Clever	Careless
Considerate	Childish
Cooperative	Coarse
Curious	Cruel
Daring	Daring
Determined	Demanding
Dutiful	Dishonest
Eager	Dull
Easygoing	Eager
Fair	Foolish
Fearless	Greedy
Friendly	Guilty
Graceful	Harsh
Helpful	Hopeless
Honest	Impolite
Hopeful	Inconsiderate
Industrious	Jealous
Innocent	Lazy
Leader	Mean
Mature	Miserable
Peaceful	Naughty
Polite	Obnoxious
Positive	
Rational	
Responsible	

Figure 3.5 A List of Character Traits for Joana

[I leave Joana with tangible artifacts to support her as she practices independently (Figures 3.4 and 3.5). At this point, I finished up my notes before moving on to another student for a conference. This also establishes clear accountability—as if to say, "I spent this time with you, we set a goal, now I'm going to follow up with you and support you as you try it." I stay for another minute to record some of my own notes (Figure 3.6).]

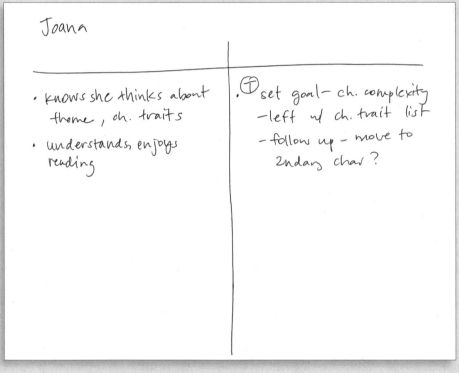

Figure 3.6 My Notes from the Conference

⬚ Wrap-Up

Every time I teach a student to synthesize, I realize how challenging this work is. Putting together many parts, seeing the overlap and the inconsistencies, and arriving at an interpretation: it is serious brain work. And, much like interpretations of your favorite book club book or

> ### *ACTION* →
>
> If you're working with Alex's work samples, imagine the conference you'd have. What would you ask? What artifacts would you gather? Are there any contrastive examples (like the rubric I provided to Joana) that would be helpful to have on hand during the conference? If you're working with a student from your own class, give this type of conferring a try.

last night's *Mad Men* episode, there isn't always one "right" answer.

What's most important in your interpretation of student data is that it's rooted in reality. Try as hard as possible not to let your preconceived notions of the student you're studying sway you away from what his work is telling you. By triangulating the data, you can be sure that the result isn't a fluke from a day that the student forgot to eat breakfast or didn't get much sleep the night before.

Before forging ahead, make sure you meet with the student in a goal-setting conference to ensure her buy-in. Having a student motivated and wanting to work on a goal will make progress and success happen much sooner than if you impose your thinking upon the student.

⬚ What's Next?

In the next chapter, we're going to explore what it takes to turn a goal into an action plan. We'll look closely at the strategies and methods you'll craft and borrow. We'll consider how you might involve others (parents, intervention specialists) in the plan and how the plan with play out over time. Finally, we'll think about clarifying an image of what it looks like when the goal is accomplished.

Chapter 4

Creating an Action Plan

Maybe I watch a bit too much HGTV, but I have to admit there is something that draws me to all of those home makeover shows. Who doesn't love seeing a dramatic positive change taking place over thirty minutes? Of course, we all know there's a great deal of planning and work that goes into that before-and-after drama. Everyone involved in the show—the designer, the carpenter, and workers—get together to analyze the situation, to make the plan, and then once they know *what* they need, they set goals. Then they shop for the materials and figure out *how* they'll transform the space.

That's what you need now—the *what* and the *how*.

This point in the process is where we take the goal of "I will clean out the garage this weekend" to the next level: a shopping trip to the Container Store, luring family members to your home with the promise of a pizza dinner, and sorting the stuff into piles of "keep, donate, toss." I'm going to be like your own private makeover host in this chapter, offering you practical strategies and methods to help you and your student turn the goal you've articulated into real, visible progress.

We have arrived at step four:

- Step 1: Collect data.
- Step 2: Analyze data.
- Step 3: Interpret data and establish a goal.

• Step 4: Create an action plan.

To me, a solid action plan needs to be able to answer a few critical *what* and *how* questions:

1. *How will I plan for repeated practice* in terms of both strategies and instructional formats?
2. *How will the teaching look over time*—who will be involved (service providers, intervention specialists, parents) and how long will it take?
3. *How will I know* when the goal has been met?

It's usually at this point when I'm explaining this protocol in a workshop that those teachers who are familiar with SMART goals from the business and management world say that this is all sounding very familiar. SMART stands for:

- S—specific
- M—measurable
- A—attainable
- R—realistic
- T—timely

And this is exactly what we're doing here. We've chosen a goal for a student that is specific and something he can attain, since it's rooted current strengths. Now we need to make a plan that is realistic. Our plan needs to be time-based and with a clear sense of what it will look like when it's been accomplished. In this way, we can begin to lead a student's work with clarity and focus.

Planning for Practice Over Time: Skills and Strategies

Once you've established a goal, there will no doubt be some skills the student will be working on to accomplish the goal. Skills may be things such as:

- reading with fluency
- inferring

- writing with more description
- visualizing
- monitoring and self-correcting

A goal may relate to one skill or to multiple skills. To keep the work focused, it is important to declare and articulate the necessary skills. However, for students to be able to practice the work and eventually become skilled, I believe they need strategies for doing so.

As mentioned earlier, researchers, authors, and theorists may disagree about the use of the terms *skill* and *strategy* (see, for example, Keene and Zimmermann 2007; Afflerbach, Pearson, and Paris 2008; Serravallo 2010; Harvey and Goudvis 2007; Wiggins 2013), and it is for that reason that I am briefly defining what *I* mean so that you can follow my points in this chapter.

To me, strategies are "deliberate, effortful, intentional and purposeful actions a [learner] takes to accomplish a specific task or skill" (Serravallo 2010, 11). The strategy is step-by-step, a procedure or recipe. But the strategy is also a scaffold. Once the reader becomes skilled, the process becomes automatic and something the reader doesn't need to give conscious attention to. The need for the strategy fades away and likely only resurfaces in times of real difficulty.

Clarifying Goals, Skills, and Strategies

Goal—Large, Overarching, Will Take Weeks to Accomplish	Skills—Behaviors, Habits, Processes	Strategies—Procedural How-tos to Accomplish the Skill
Understand that stories have deeper, thematic meanings.	• Interpreting • Inferring • Synthesizing	Often authors have a lesson in mind when writing a story. To uncover that lesson, it's helpful to look at the end of the story to see what a character has learned, and then consider what you as a reader should have learned as well.

continues

Goal—Large, Overarching, Will Take Weeks to Accomplish	Skills—Behaviors, Habits, Processes	Strategies—Procedural How-tos to Accomplish the Skill
Understand that stories have deeper, thematic meanings.	• Planning story ideas with theme in mind	When coming up with an idea for a story, it is sometimes helpful to think about social issues in our lives—class, race, gender—and then think, "What is it I want my story to say about that issue?" Then, plan a story where the character learns the lesson you want your reader to learn.
Monitor for meaning and fix up mistakes closer to the point of error.	• Monitoring for meaning	When writing, reread as you go. Track the words with your finger as you reread to ensure you aren't missing any words. When reading, ask yourself "Did that make sense, sound right, and look right?" If something doesn't, go back and fix it.
Work with more attention and focus during reading and writing workshops.	• Choosing just-right books • Self-monitoring engagement • Refocusing • Visualizing	Look back across the last few weeks' worth of book logs. Notice the books you abandoned and those you stuck with. What are the patterns? Find books with similar traits as those you liked.

Goal—Large, Overarching, Will Take Weeks to Accomplish	Skills—Behaviors, Habits, Processes	Strategies—Procedural How-tos to Accomplish the Skill
	• Building stamina	In longer books, set short-term goals for yourself. Place a sticky note or bookmark every certain number of pages (the number will vary based on what the reader considers appropriate). When you get to the sticky note, check yourself. Did you understand what you read? Did you stay focused?

Where Do I Find the Strategies I Need?

When speaking to teachers at workshops or conferences, I often get asked "So, Jen, can you just give us a list of the strategies we need to teach?"

Here's the thing: there really is no list of "the" strategies. Most of the ones I teach kids, I make up. That's right—they didn't come from a teacher's guide or discrete source. I made them up by reflecting on my own processes as a reader or writer and articulating them as a series of steps.

Afflerbach, Pearson, and Paris (2008) assert in their article on skills and strategies that "Skills are automatic processes, strategies are deliberately controlled" (368). This means that in order to teach a student a skill that you already possess as an adult, proficient reader and writer, you need to apply a bit of metacognition to articulate the steps. For some, this is easiest when we put ourselves in a situation of challenge. In working through the challenge, the underground, automatic skill becomes more visible. For example, to help a student who needs work decoding multisyllabic words, you could try to get through a science journal article that would have many opportunities for you to practice your own decoding. If the child's working on better understanding theme, maybe you'll think about how you interpreted the last novel you read for your Thursday night book club.

When you make your own strategies, they will be authentic, in language you're comfortable with, and easier to demonstrate. You'll know what you meant. Sometimes when teachers borrow others' language, they find it hard to pull off, they stumble over their words, or the demonstration doesn't quite match what they said they were demonstrating.

While my first answer is always to reflect and make your own for the reasons above, it is true that you can go to a number of resources to find sample strategies (see sidebar on this page). I would caution against using these as merely "the list" and instead think of them as a bank of examples.

Before rushing to one of the resources mentioned in the sidebar, try out the process of developing your own strategies by reflecting on your own reading. Read "The Real Princess," the short story by Hans Christian Anderson, in Figure 4.1. As you read, try to think about the characters in the story. Notice what you do to develop those ideas and thoughts.

What ideas do you have about the Queen? How about the Princess? Perhaps you think that the Queen-mother was the one in control in the family. Or maybe that the Prince was a spoiled brat, or perhaps that the Princess was innocent and naïve.

Or any number of other potential thoughts and reactions.

Now, reflect on how it is that you came upon those ideas. If you had to articulate a process you went through, what would you say it is? Perhaps what you did was hone in on one piece of particularly compelling dialogue and/or action that really revealed something about the character. For example, when the Queen says "Ah! We shall soon see that!" perhaps you thought "She's so distrustful" and when she set up the mattress test perhaps you thought "If the prince wants a princess so badly, why doesn't he do the test? I guess Mom's in charge at that castle."

Resources for finding sample strategies:

- *Units of Study for Teaching Reading, Grades 3–5* (Calkins, Tolan, and Ehrenworth 2010)

- *How's It Going?* (Anderson 2000)

- *Units of Study in Opinion, Information, and Narrative Writing* (Calkins and colleagues 2013)

- *Curricular Plans for the Reading and Writing Workshop, Grades K–8* (Calkins and colleagues 2011)

- *Teaching Reading in Small Groups* (Serravallo 2010)

- *Independent Reading Assessment: Fiction* (Serravallo 2012)

- *Independent Reading Assessment: Nonfiction* (Serravallo 2013)

- *Conferring with Readers* (Serravallo and Goldberg 2007)

The Real Princess
by Hans Christian Anderson

There was once a Prince who wished to marry a Princess; but then she must be a real Princess. He travelled all over the world in hopes of finding such a lady; but there was always something wrong. Princesses he found in plenty; but whether they were real Princesses it was impossible for him to decide, for now one thing, now another, seemed to him not quite right about the ladies. At last he returned to his palace quite cast down, because he wished so much to have a real Princess for his wife.

One evening a fearful tempest arose, it thundered and lightened, and the rain poured down from the sky in torrents: besides, it was as dark as pitch. All at once there was heard a violent knocking at the door, and the old King, the Prince's father, went out himself to open it.

It was a Princess who was standing outside the door. What with the rain and the wind, she was in a sad condition; the water trickled down from her hair, and her clothes clung to her body. She said she was a real Princess.

"Ah! We shall soon see that!" thought the old Queen-mother; however, she said not a word of what she was going to do; but went quietly into the bedroom, took all the bed-clothes off the bed, and put three little peas on the bedstead. She then laid twenty mattresses one upon another over the three peas, and put twenty feather beds over the mattresses.

Upon this bed the Princess was to pass the night.

The next morning she was asked how she had slept. "Oh, very badly indeed!" she replied. "I have scarcely closed my eyes the whole night through. I do not know what was in my bed, but I had something hard under me, and am all over black and blue. It has hurt me so much!"

Now it was plain that the lady must be a real Princess, since she had been able to feel the three little peas through the twenty mattresses and twenty feather beds. None but a real Princess could have had such a delicate sense of feeling.

The Prince accordingly made her his wife; being now convinced that he had found a real Princess. The three peas were however put into the cabinet of curiosities, where they are still to be seen, provided they are not lost.

Wasn't this a lady of real delicacy?

Figure 4.1

So, to develop a strategy, you now need to articulate your process in terms that are not specific to the story. Perhaps your strategy would be something like, "Notice a place where the character is speaking or acting. Think to yourself, what kind of person would speak like that? Act like that? Use character traits to describe your character."

ACTION ⟶

Try to come up with a few more strategies, using the "Real Princess" or another text you have handy. Try another skill—for example, try retelling the text. Ask yourself how you were able to do it. Name your process as a sequence of steps. You may also want to try coming up with a few informational text strategies about how you determine the main idea, understand key details, get meaning from text features, or figure out unknown vocabulary.

A strategy for developing strategies:

1. Put yourself in a situation where you have the opportunity to practice the skill for which you're trying to develop a strategy.
2. Spy on yourself as you read and think.
3. Articulate what you did—your process—into a series of generalizable steps.

So . . . What's the Plan for Joana?

Remember that Joana's goal is to focus more on character development in her writing, and character analysis in her reading (especially secondary characters).

Some of the skills she'll work to develop are:

- inferring
- elaborating/writing with detail
- revising

Keep in mind that she'll be working on this goal for a while, over time. Over the course of the next few weeks, I'll introduce strategies that I think best fit where she is in the journey toward reaching her goal and ones that best match the reading and writing units of study going on in the classroom. Some of the strategies I might teach her are:

- Inferring: Notice how a secondary character has an impact on the main character by comparing how a character acts in the presence of secondary characters.
- Inferring: Create a character web of the main and secondary characters. Draw lines between each of the characters and write how they affect each other, act in each other's presence, or impact change on the other character.

- Writing with details that show, not tell: Think about the character's trait that is especially important in this moment in your story. Think, "How would someone like that speak to another person?" Look back at your dialogue and revise, considering the character's trait.
- Writing with detail: Before drafting a fiction story, develop a character in your notebook. Think about a character's hope, dreams, wants, obstacles, and inner traits and external traits. Make sure that the character is multidimensional, not flat. Plan to include this development when you draft.
- Revision: Look back at scenes you've written where characters interact. Look at what you've written about what a character says and does. Can you tell that the pre-writing work you've done developing the character shows up in the story? If not, make changes that reflect the character's traits as you planned them.

ACTION →

Think about the goal you have for Alex or your chosen student. Identify the skills that will help him accomplish the goal. Brainstorm a few strategies that will help the student access those goals. My thoughts on Alex are in Appendix A.

Planning for Practice Over Time: Instructional Formats and Methods

In order for a student to accomplish a goal, she needs repeated practice with skills and strategies and a decreased level of support over time. The role of the teacher is to constantly assess where the student is in relation to the eventual goal and to provide instruction that stretches, but doesn't overwhelm, the student. Working within the student's zone of proximal development ensures that your teaching is consistently building on a strength as opposed to teaching to a deficit (Vygotsky 1978).

If the strategy offered to the student, and the work required of the student, is a stretch beyond what she is already doing, chances are good the student will need some support. *Scaffolding*, a term first used in developmental literature by Wood, Brunner, and Ross (1976), was later applied to educational contexts to refer to the support a teacher provides to a student learning a new competency.

Like the scaffolds around a building under construction, instructional scaffolds are temporary and need to be removed over time. This "gradual release of responsibility" is often accomplished by choosing instructional formats and methods that at first offer the student a great deal of support, and then over time expect that the student takes on more of the work with less and less teacher input (Pearson and Gallagher 1983). See Figure 4.2.

Instructional Formats and Degrees of Support

High	Moderate	Low
Minilesson	Shared reading	Independent reading
Interactive read-aloud	Strategy lessons	Partnerships/book clubs
Close reading	Conferring	Peer editing

Figure 4.2

On a microlevel, we can also study how we interact with students *within* each instructional format. For example, it's possible to teach a read-aloud that has a great deal of support—with the teacher doing a lot of thinking aloud, stopping often to prompt student thinking with a lot of support, offering opportunities for students to converse as they make sense of the text, as well as little support—reading a story straight through without stopping.

In *Teaching Reading in Small Groups* (2010), I wrote about considering how much support you offer students before, during, and after a lesson. Before, for example, you have the option to demonstrate, give an example, or just offer the strategy. During the guided practice, you can offer each student a range of support from elaborate prompts that offer a lot of support to nonverbal cues that put more responsibility on the student (see Figure 4.3).

Fisher and Frey, in their 2008 book *Better Learning Through Structured Teaching*, offer a helpful diagram to conceptualize the gradually diminishing role of the teacher and the increased role of the student (see Figure 4.4).

In the sections that follow, I offer a brief description of some instructional formats that you may choose to use as you go about planning for instruction over time with your student. I review structures that I use most often when working with students individually or in small groups. I have chosen not to describe whole-class teaching structures; however, minilessons and read-alouds would be excellent choices if you find that most of your class needs the same work as the student you're currently focusing on.

Three Levels of Decision Making to Move Children Toward Independence

Before Coached Practice	During Coached Practice	Over Time
What method will you use?	How supportive will your prompts be?	• How many times will you see the readers in the group?
• Demonstration		
	• Heavy	• How will you use leaner supports over time?
• Shared practice		
	• Medium	
• Example/explanation		• How will you support transference to new books?
	• Lean	
• State strategy		

Figure 4.3

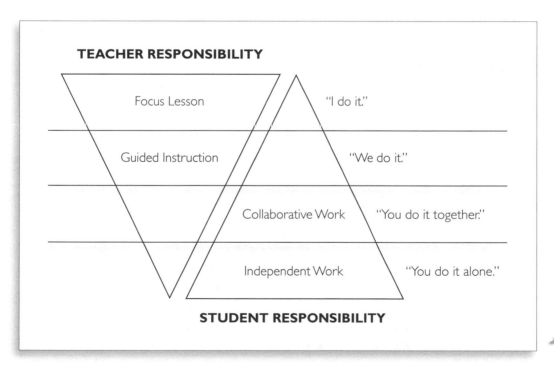

Figure 4.4 Over time, teachers should work to lessen their level of support and require more independence from the student. Different instructional formats can be chosen purposefully to offer varying levels of support.

Keep in mind your goal of releasing responsibility to the student by choosing structures that offer the most amount of support initially and then easing into structures that require the least amount of support gradually over time. In addition, keep in mind that you can vary your level of support within the lesson based on how near the student is to accomplishing the goal.

While the list of instructional formats I've chosen to include in this chapter is by no means all-inclusive, I do think they represent those I most commonly used as a classroom teacher and those I most frequently recommend to teachers in grades 3 to 6. It may have struck you that I've chosen not to include word study and guided reading. I did so because I find that these structures have greater application when working toward a goal for a kindergarten, first-, or second-grade learner. If you have a student who is performing on more of a primary elementary level, you may want to consult the companion book to this one for grades K–2.

In the sections that follow I explain instructional formats. At the end of this chapter, I walk through how I would decide which of these formats to use with Joana and how I would plan to use them over time.

Conferring

Individual conferences offer the opportunity for a teacher to sit with a student to learn about him, establish and follow-up on goals, hold him accountable for prior work, and offer guided practice with current work.

Within a reading workshop, students are reading different self-selected books at different reading levels. During writing workshop, students are writing their own pieces on different topics. Conferring allows me to see each student as an individual learner and teach each child strategies that best match her. The strategies I choose to teach are aligned to the goal I've chosen, and the level of support I provide during the conference matches where the child is in his own progress toward independent practice of the goal.

Most conferences follow a predictable structure that allows me as the teacher to make effective use of my time—both within the single conference and across my entire class. If I spend too long with one student, offering a high level of support, not only have I spent time working on something the student will need my presence to continue practicing, but the other students in the class have been robbed of instructional time. Without being too strict, I try to keep my eye on the clock and aim for a conference to last no more than about five minutes. Some will be a little shorter, some a little longer, but on average five minutes is what I'm aiming for.

The structure that I use most is known as the "research-decide-teach" conference (Calkins 2000; Anderson 2000; Calkins, Hartman, and White 2005; Serravallo and Goldberg 2007). Using this structure, I first attempt to learn about what strategies the student is currently using and needs to learn. Next, I chose a specific teaching point for the conference. Then, I support the student in practicing the strategy. Finally, I wrap up by reminding the student of my expectations for her continued work.

....

CONFERRING STRUCTURE:

Research: Ask questions, observe, listen to the child read, investigate artifacts (sticky notes, reading logs, reading notebook). Keeping in mind the goal you've established and all you already know about the reader, notice how the student's current work reflects your prior assessments and the goal you established. Plan to spend about one minute of the five researching.

Decide: Decide on a compliment and teaching point. Ideally the compliment will be a segue to the teaching point. This ensures that you're teaching to strengthen a strength as opposed to responding to a perceived deficit.

Compliment: Offer the student a clear, explicit compliment. Being as specific as possible, tell the student what he has done well, *why* it's important, and offer an example of what he did that shows evidence of the strength. Being specific and elaborate with your compliment ensures that the student can replicate the skill or behavior—which is sometimes something he didn't even realize he was doing.

Teach: Offer the student a specific strategy that she can practice to take the next step beyond what she is already doing. Say the strategy in clear, specific language. Depending on how much support the student needs, you may choose to give an example or offer a brief demonstration. Give the student a chance to practice with your support, as needed. Offer coaching prompts and questions. This is the longest part of the conference, lasting about two to three minutes.

Link: Repeat your teaching from today's conference, referring to how the work of today relates to the overarching goal you've established. At this point in the conference, I often find it helpful to establish a clear expectation for follow-up. I clarify what I expect the student to do before our next meeting and often give the student a tangible reminder of the strategy. Often I record the teaching point on a sticky note or a bookmark or note on a page of the student's reading or writing notebook. This will be quick—less than a minute.

Small-Group Strategy Lessons

In 2010, I wrote *Teaching Reading in Small Groups* with the goal of offering more than a dozen types of small-group instruction formats that may be chosen as an alternative to guided reading to match the myriad purposes that arise in a given classroom. Perhaps the most common and versatile of these is the small-group strategy lesson. They are versatile because I can use them in reading or writing, for any skill or behavior that I want to reinforce.

Strategy lessons offer an opportunity for students to practice new strategies or review strategies they've learned before. Within the small group, the students all practice the same strategy while the teacher moves around, supporting each individual student at his entry point. It is for this reason that I also refer to strategy lessons as "group conferences"—I try to maintain the same individualized feel as a one-on-one conference.

Strategy lessons, like all the other structures I mention in this chapter, follow a predictable structure that help teachers to plan, help children to know their responsibilities, and allow everyone to make the best use of time during the lesson.

While the other students are reading or writing independently, I begin the lesson by establishing the focus for our seven to ten minutes together. I state the strategy in clear language and offer a visual (chart or icons) aid if I think it would support the students. I try to get students working as quickly as possible—within ninety seconds or so—and then begin to make my way around the group. Like a plate spinner in the circus, trying to keep plates up on the end of sticks before they drop, I try to keep each student working productively as I move quickly among them. As I move from student to student, I offer feedback and support to appropriately nudge each student toward independent practice of the strategy. At the end, I repeat the strategy either as a whole-group lesson or on an individual basis.

....

STRATEGY LESSON STRUCTURE:

Connect and compliment: Begin the lesson by establishing a clear purpose and a connection to the ongoing work of their goal. This is a great time to remind students of their goal and/or to remind them how the work they will do in reading relates to writing or vice versa. Whenever possible, I also try to offer a compliment to reinforce a common strength. Keep this quick— about thirty seconds.

Teach: After a quick introduction, I state the teaching point, or strategy, for the day's lesson. Depending on how new the strategy is, I decide on the level of up-front support. For example, if this is the first time they've heard the strategy, I'm likely to provide a brief demonstration where I read or write as well as model my thinking. If they've tried the strategy before, I may offer less support in the form of a quick example or explanation. If this is a strategy that the children have practiced many times before, I'll probably just state the strategy and then get them working right away.

Actively engage: By now, the lesson is about ninety seconds in. I'm now going to offer differentiated, individualized support as I move from student to student in the group. Spending thirty to sixty seconds with each student, I make my way around, coaching as they practice. I often quickly assess and then offer feedback in the form of prompts. Prompts may be questions, directives, redirections, or even compliments.

Link: Before students return to independent reading or writing, I want to send the message that they should continue practicing without my support until we meet again. I either speak to each student individually or I call all of the students' attention back together. I choose the individual route if I tweaked the teaching point for individuals during the active engagement section. If the coaching support I provided was pretty consistent across students, I repeat the teaching point to all of them. As in a conference, here is where I often tell students what I expect for them to do between now and when I see them again, and I often give the students some sort of a tangible reminder to focus them as they continue to practice on their own. This is a quick wrap-up, lasting less than a minute.

Book Clubs and Partnerships, and Conferring During Talk

Book clubs and partnerships offer students experience with an essential ingredient to being an engaged, lifelong reader: the ability to have social interactions around books. Great conversations can invigorate children, spark new thinking, encourage laughter, and teach about healthy debate. They can help students come to new insights and even increase motivation to read.

Book clubs and partnerships rarely go well without some instruction, however. Children need to learn how to have productive conversations, period, and when the talk is focused on books, a child's comprehension (or lack thereof) also comes into play.

Most teachers committed to a reading workshop approach agree that giving students several opportunities each week to talk about books is important and worth the time. Many teachers find time during the time of day they've carved out for read-aloud to give students time to talk in partners or groups or as a whole class. During this time, teachers act as coaches who prompt, give feedback, and offer teaching points to help move the conversation along (Serravallo 2010; Nichols 2006; Calkins 2000).

In addition to the time during read-aloud, reading workshop can offer opportunities for children to choose common texts, read those texts alone preparing for conversation by writing about their reading, and then discuss the books and their thinking with peers. While students talk, the teacher often circulates around the room, offering suggestions to each group. These are opportunities to confer during talk.

When conferring during talk, I tend to follow a structure.

When I first arrive at a club's conversation, I listen to students talk without interrupting to ask my own questions. I stay on the periphery, taking notes in the form of a quick transcript. As I write, I'm thinking about two main categories: What might I teach to support these students' *conversational* skills? What might I teach to support these students' *comprehension* skills? Of course, both the conversational and comprehension skills relate back to the students' individualized goals for reading.

When I've decided what to teach, I use one of four methods: ghost partner, proficient partner, example and explanation, or demonstration.

- With ghost partner, I whisper prompts and sentence starters into students' ears, encouraging them to reuse my language with the club. All of the prompts I whisper focus on a specific teaching point.
- With proficient partner, I join the club, acting as a member of the club. With this method, I offer ideas and questions to keep the conversation going.
- With example and explanation or demonstration, I treat it more like a strategy lesson—stating a clear teaching point and showing them what I mean. In all instances, I wrap up by repeating my teaching with a link.

....

A SUGGESTED STRUCTURE FOR CONFERRING DURING CONVERSATION:

Research: Listen to student conversation without interrupting. While I may have questions in my mind that beg for clarification, I try to only go on what I'm hearing the students say. Interrupting them to ask questions disrupts the flow of conversation.

Decide: As I listen, I try to decide on a teaching point. I think about conversational skills and comprehension skills. As with any type of conferring, I look to strengthen strengths, not teach to deficits. I keep the student's goals in mind as I select a compliment and a teaching point.

Compliment: Offer students a clear, concrete compliment. It's helpful to state their strength, why it's a strength, and an example of the strength.

Teach: I chose one of four methods: ghost partner, proficient partner, example/explanation, or demonstration. Staying focused on just one strategy, I either coach by whispering in students' ears, joining the conversation, or showing and telling the strategy, respectively.

Link: Before leaving the group to continue talking without me there, I repeat the teaching point for today's lesson. I establish accountability by reminding them that I'll look for their practice the next time I see them.

Writing Clubs and Partnerships

In her 2004 *Independent Writing*, M. Colleen Cruz talks about the importance of community to a developing writer. Writers need other writers who know their struggles and triumphs and who can support them along all steps of the writing process. In writing groups (also known as "colonies," "workshops," "clubs," or "salons"), writers may critique, compliment, and offer advice and support.

In many classrooms I visit, teachers have paired students up as writing partners with good intentions. But sometimes, feeling the pressure of so much to cover in so little time, teachers only have students meet once in a while—usually at the end of the process, for peer editing. But as Cruz reminds us, there is so much more that can happen during these writing groups. When a student's goal involves anything from doing more planning before writing, being more intentional and purposeful about revision, or studying mentor authors to improve craft, a writing club or partnership can be a great support.

These partnerships and clubs can be permanent or temporary arrangements. Students need to prepare for the conversation by bringing a sample of their writing to share and/or a question they want answered. Typically, a group follows some protocol. For example, students can decide to share an excerpt of writing and then hear feedback. Or, the writer can decide to pose a problem to the group, then read the writing, and hear suggestions. Teachers can play an important role in the club's meetings by helping students ask probing questions and teaching them how to offer critique that is constructive. Teachers may also help to focus students on their particular goal and help them craft questions of the rest of the club that will help lend insight toward improvement with that goal.

Close Reading

It is helpful to teach children to read closely when their goal involves careful and deliberate examination of details in a text. It is carefully planned with students and strategies in mind. The teacher often balances thinking aloud and guiding questions to help students uncover deeper meanings in the text. It is a helpful structure to use when a student's goal centers around inference, interpretation, and/or studying author's craft. Since my work with Joana would be around deeper comprehension, this might be a great format to use with her.

The questioning that teachers plan during a close reading lesson often includes the goal of helping awaken a student reader's own inquisitive nature. That is, the teacher shouldn't be teaching the *text* but instead teaching transferrable questions and strategies. Questions are generally open-ended and text-dependent, not questions where you as the teacher already know the sole "correct" answer. These questions ideally help students have conversations with one another, not simply engage in a teacher-student-teacher-student volley (see Figure 4.5).

The approach you teach in a close reading lesson is not one you would want readers to follow every time they read. Doing so might cause the reading to become slow, laborious, or tedious. Instead, the reader is learning techniques for reading closely that she may apply during times when deeper analysis of the text is called for.

Close reading lessons are best focused on short, complex texts that are rich with possible layers of meaning. Therefore, careful text selection is crucial. Since this lesson type involves a real slowing down and

---

Defining the Term

The term *close reading* has become popular with the adoption of the Common Core in many states. The idea of close reading isn't new; many of us probably engaged in this kind of reading in college and high school. The idea that students are taught to read slowly and carefully and to annotate thinking as they go is likely a new idea for many elementary school teachers.

One of the goals of close reading in elementary school is to bring greater rigor to reading, both in the types of thinking we draw students' attention to and in the high level of complexity in the texts we select. While I am all for students improving their skills as readers, I want to caution about overdoing close reading in grades 3, 4, and 5. Use caution when borrowing premade lessons you can find in textbooks or by googling "close reading" on the Internet. Please always keep in mind what we know from Piaget (Elkind 1976; Vygotsky 1978) and work in ways that empower students, not make them feel inadequate or incapable as readers.

---

acute attention, it's often challenging to maintain the engagement of an eight- to eleven-year-old. Therefore, I try to choose a very short text—a self-contained text or excerpt from a longer text, no more than about eight hundred words or one to two pages in total.

Questions to Elicit Deep Thinking During Close Reading Lessons

Use Open-Ended Questions to Prompt Discussion, Such As:	Avoid Questions with a Clear Correct Answer, Such As:
• What do you think the author meant when she said ___?	• What are three types of migrating birds?
• The text says ____, but we know from another text that _____. What are you thinking now?	• What is the first detail in this section?
	• Who is the author of this text?
• Why would the author have chosen the word _____ to use in this part?	• List three things you learned from reading this text.
• From whose perspective is this story being told?	• How many …?
	• Who is …?
• I'm noticing the author is using a lot of short sentences in this part. What effect does this craft decision have on the tone of the piece?	• What is …?
	• Where is …?

Figure 4.5

Another consideration to keep in mind when deciding whether to choose close reading lessons for your students is your own response to the debate about where meaning lies within a text. The writers of the Common Core are championing "text-dependent" questions and analysis, with the idea that the meaning in a text lies within the text itself. For decades, many have argued that it is in fact a reader's response to the text that determines the meaning. (See, for example, Fisher, Frey, and Lapp 2012; Beers and Probst 2012; Rosenblatt 1994.) My own view is that there needs to be a middle ground between the two interpretations. Deciding on what you believe will help you craft questions to guide your own students' thinking.

Texts selected for this type of instruction are generally referred to as "grade-level complex texts," meaning that they are above the level a reader can easily handle independently. For Joana, who reads independently at level R, I might select a text at level T.

The teacher plays a crucial role in providing support. In addition, since a teacher's goal in doing this type of lesson is often deeper comprehension work like inference and analyzing author craft, students benefit from having teachers support students in determining where to stop and think and what to stop and think about. This is a highly scaffolded lesson type, and therefore students likely derive much more meaning from the text than they would on their own.

What follows is a possible structure for the lesson, adapted from Beers and Probst (2012). You may think that this is similar to a read-aloud, with four important differences. One is that the reading is done from a single copy of a text (on a SMART Board, chart, or overhead projection) so that all students can read along together. In a read-aloud, only the teacher sees the text. The second difference is that there is likely to be more stopping to think aloud and prompt students with questions. Third, texts chosen for this lesson type need to be very short, while length of texts for read-aloud can vary. Finally, rereading plays a very important role in close reading lessons, as a first read rarely leads to the depth of thinking we're after in a close reading lesson.

For more information about close reading lessons, see:

- *Text Complexity* (Fisher, Frey, and Lapp 2012), which clearly describes model close reading lessons at various grade levels

- *Notice and Note* (Beers and Probst 2012), which focuses on close reading lessons and lenses to use when studying literary texts

- *Falling in Love with Close Reading* (Lehman and Roberts 2013)

- Rosenblatt (1994), which puts forth the reading-response theory

A SUGGESTED CLOSE READING LESSON STRUCTURE:

Introduce a technique, tip, or concept: Introducing a transferrable teaching point or strategy before students practice will help encourage transfer. Explain up front what you want them to understand about the reading process, not just what you want them to understand about the text you've chosen. After stating the transferrable work, you may choose to explain, give an example, or even do a very brief demonstration.

Apply: Read together (in chorus) from a single copy of a text. Avoid making copies and distributing them so each student has his own—this can lead students to read ahead or become disengaged or distracted. When you have all eyes in the same place, you'll better be able to manage everyone's attention. As you read, balance think-alouds and questions to engage students in their own thinking and conversation with one another.

Review: Reinforce the tip(s) or technique(s) you applied so that students may transfer this learning to their independent reading.

ACTION →

Consider Alex or the student from your class you've chosen to make a plan for. Which of the instructional formats described in this chapter might be a good fit for your student? Think about the purposes of each when making your decision. Jot down some plans.

So . . . What's the Plan for Joana?

In reading workshop, I would plan to use a blend of all of the methods described in this chapter.

I would put Joana into a book club with other students who would enjoy some character-driven novels. I would plan to offer her club a short list of novels that lend themselves to the type of character analysis she'll be practicing. During their conversations, I'd coach them to notice and discuss secondary characters and push them to do deeper analysis.

I'd use strategy lessons (when other children could benefit from the same work) and conferring to introduce strategies during reading and writing. I'd treat these as a series of individualized lessons, reteaching lessons with a gradually diminishing level of teacher support.

Since she reads at a level toward the upper end of her grade level, I'd use close reading as a lesson structure with her and another small group of students who are around the same level. This way, the text will be accessible to all of them. In these groups, I can integrate her goal with the goal(s) of the other students in her group.

⬜ **Practice Over Time: Involving Others**

One of the most significant hurdles to making timely progress with a goal is when the work a student is told to do and/or the teaching he or she receives is muddled and confused. When a student receives mixed messages about what to focus on, the end result is often that the child focuses on none of it.

Students who qualify for intervention are often the students who are most vulnerable to this confusion. These students are pulled out during class time or work with specialists who "push in" during literacy periods. In either case, these interventionists often have made their own plans for the student. By virtue of the fact that a teacher's day is overscheduled and busy as it is, these interventionists and classroom teachers rarely have time to sit down with each another. While it may be true that everything each teacher teaches is helpful to the student, it's probably also true that focusing on *the most important* work and being a united front yields faster progress and less confusion on the part of the learner.

Add this within-school challenge to the home–school connection challenge. At times, students go home to parents or caregivers who have different ideas about what good schoolwork looks like or what is most important to pay attention to. In one school where I taught for three years, most parents seemed very concerned with handwriting and spelling above all else. While I agree it's important for children to learn proper letter formation and to spell in ways that allow their writing to be read by others, it was only in maybe one case where I would have agreed that those were the *most important* areas to focus on. So another question to consider is, "How will you make the student's goal clear to the adults the child goes home to each night?"

Although teacher's workloads are only becoming more taxing, there may be ways to put systems in place to communicate among the adults involved. One idea is to have a communication sheet with a goal at the top of the page and places to add strategies and tools, as well as ongoing note taking (see Figure 4.6).

Within the school, this can be kept in a two-pocket folder by the front door of the classroom in a basket. Whenever a reading specialist or English as a second language teacher comes to pick up a student for intervention, the routine could be that he takes the folder with him, reviews

Dear Petrika _____

___Joana_____ and I have recently had a conversation to set goals for the coming weeks of reading and writing. Goals help us to have a focus and intention when practicing reading and writing at home and at school. We wanted to let you know about our conversation so that you can provide support as well.

Reading Goal:	Writing Goal:
See characters – main and secondary – as complex.	Develop complex characters and show the traits in stories she creates.

We expect that with daily practice, the goals will be accomplished on or around ___6/20___
Here are some ways you can help ___Joana_____ at home:

Reading	Writing
·Ask J. about the characters in her books. ·Talk about characters on T.V. shows you watch together. ·Read aloud stories with great characters ·check out the resources (like the traits list) I send home.	·make up stories together ·Notice people on the subway and talk about how you'd describe them if they were characters in a story you wrote.

I welcome your thoughts and feedback!

Sincerely,

Ms. S

May be photocopied for classroom use © 2013 by Jennifer Serravallo from The Literacy Teacher's Playbook, Grades 3-6. Portsmouth, NH: Heinemann.

Figure 4.6 Note-Taking Form for Communicating with Other Adults About Students' Goals (A blank form is provided in Appendix C.)

the most current strategies taught and notes taken, and then teaches in a way that aligns to the message the student has already been getting within the classroom. Then, at the end of the thirty-minute session, the reading specialist would also jot down his own notes about the student's work during that period and would return the folder to its spot by the door. If every classroom in a school had this sort of system, the cross-classroom communication could be streamlined, and a student could receive more consistent instruction (see Figure 4.7).

Teachers could also adopt a home–school connection system. In my work in many different schools, I've seen different systems work well. In one school, the last page of the reading and writing notebooks are reserved for teaching notes. After a conference or small-group lesson, the student dates and records *her own understanding* of the teaching that took place during that lesson. Notebooks go home each night and parents could then see the teaching that happened.

Joshua   Writing: use varied detail with purpose

Who	Date	Strengths	Teaching Possibilities
Janice (speech)	3/30	• Using dialogue • Some action ©details	• purposeful dialogue • more detailed (T) action
Mrs. White	4/3	©. revised to write w/ more detailed action	(T) slow down the action by visualizing the scene
Janice	4/6		• Storytelling with coaching to add in more precise details. (action)
Mrs. White	4/9	• © Details look good (action) -	(T). convo. about how to show ch. traits through dialogue. Practical revising.

Figure 4.7 One example of a note-taking form that can be used across instructional environments, i.e., by both the classroom teacher and pull-out intervention support teachers. (A blank version is provided in Appendix C.)

To many parents, reading and writing workshops are hard to understand because there is no textbook and there are no tests. Because of this, many parents feel disconnected from the curriculum and the individualized teaching that happens with their child in the classroom. Some system—in a notebook, on paper, through ongoing emails or in-person conferences—can help parents to feel part of the process.

So . . . What's the Plan for Joana?

Joana does not qualify for any intervention, so the only area for consistency to consider in her case is the home–school connection. Joana happens to have very involved parents who I think would welcome being included in plans for her and who could be counted on to follow up on the work she does within the classroom.

When reading books together at home, or even when watching television, I would suggest that Joana and her parents discuss the characters from a writing or author's craft perspective and a reading perspective. One idea is to send

ACTION →

Make plans for involving others for Alex or the student you've chosen from your class. If you've chosen Alex, be aware that he is seen by a speech therapist thirty minutes twice a week and a reading intervention teacher thirty minutes each day out of the classroom.

home some questions they can ask her about the book she's reading. These questions may be similar questions that I would introduce to her book club. For example:

- What kind of person is _____?
- How is ____ affecting ____?
- What did the writer do to make you think that about the character?
- Can you see this character in more than one way?
- Is there a place in this show/book where the character acted out of character?
- Why did the author include this character?
- What did the author do to make these two characters different?

I would also plan to have Joana take notes in the back of both her reading and writing notebooks about the ongoing work we do during conferences, book clubs, close reading lessons, and small-group strategy lessons. I'd ask her to take her notebooks home at least once a week to share her work with her parents.

❑ Practice Over Time: Planning for Multiple Students and Across a Week

For several weeks ahead, you and the student you studied will meet in the variety of instructional formats that you planned. As you meet, you introduce new strategies when needed.

I find that typically a student needs a few opportunities of guided practice with a strategy. This guided practice could be in a conference, small-group setting, book club, or other structure. When a student "gets it" the very first time I teach it, I usually feel that the teaching might not have reached far enough.

Once a student develops a level of automaticity with a strategy, I introduce a new strategy—still keeping in mind the focus of the goal we've established. For example, if Joana starts to do well with a writing strategy of planning characters to be multidimensional by thinking of traits that help the character overcome obstacles and traits that stand in the way of the character overcoming obstacles, then I might move on to a new strategy. At that point, I might ask her to work on revising her draft by making sure she's showing and not telling the character's traits. She might do this by revising the character's actions, dialogue, and internal thinking.

In other words, the strategies can build upon each other, each strategy offering a new level of depth.

Each week as you plan your whole-class, small-group, and individual instruction, it's a good idea to revisit any notes you took during your work with the student. Using these notes will help you consider when to move on to new teaching and when to revisit a previously taught strategy.

Once you take the ideas in this book to scale and have a clearly set goal for each student in your class, you'll use this master class list of goals to help you decide on your approach for the week. To transfer a list of student names into a weekly plan, I typically start with groups, then move on to individuals. Looking at my class list, I follow a process such as this:

1. I ask myself, "Which students have similar goals and are at about the same reading/writing level?" I then group those students and put them into the "strategy lesson" row, and put a check mark next to their names to indicate that I have a plan for them.
2. I ask myself, "Which student's goals lend themselves to work during partnership/club/conversation time?" and I plan to see them during the two or three days a week where I have set aside time during conversation.
3. I ask myself, "Which students have goals that are somewhat unique?" Those students are ones that I plan to see one-on-one in conferences.
4. I ask myself, "Whom should I be sure to check in with more than once?" and I make it a point to repeat a strategy lesson and/or conference. I may also leave in buffer time for myself at the end of the workshop for playing catch-up and/or for checking in quickly with students who've recently met with me.

In the example in Figure 4.8 you can see the class at a glance, and in Figure 4.9 you can see my plan for the week. Notice that I've grouped Mark, Jasmine, and Shanique because they had similar goals. I planned to see Vanessa and Nick during book club time because their goals lent themselves to work during conversation. Students such as Mercer, Isabelle, and Jakson are slated to see me during conferring time since their goals are somewhat different from their peers.

ACTION →

Using the template in Appendix C, page 165, or one you create yourself based on Figure 4.9, create a weekly plan for your class. If you're working with Alex's data, you can use Figure 4.8 to create an alternate weekly plan.

Figure 4.9 This Week-at-a-Glance Sheet (find a blank version in Appendix C) helps to create a schedule to ensure that most students meet with the teacher at least twice within a week.

Planning Your Week

	Monday	Tuesday	Wednesday	Thursday	Friday
Strategy Lesson (10 min)		Sunniva? Mei Ling Mateo ⑩ vocab./ fig. lang	TBD ⑩		Caroline M.? Alex elab. in W abt. R ⑩
Strategy Lesson (10 min)	Joana J.? Rajiv T.} 2ndary charact. ⑩	Mark Jasmine? Shanique} traits ⑩	Joana J.? Rajiv T.} apply to talk? ⑩		Mark? Jasmine Shanique} traits ⑩
Conferences (5 minutes each)	Mercer N. ⑤	Isabelle W. ⑤ Jakson L.— goal-setting conf.	Mai Ling H. ⑤ Alex — goal-setting	Kesla A. ⑤ Jakson L. ⑤ Rachel S. ⑤ Francine S. ⑤	? ⑤ ? ⑤ ? ⑤ ? ⑤
Guided Reading (15–20 min)					
Other (15 min) Book clubs	Vanessa K. ⑮ Eliot P. Latcesha B. Theo Z.			Nick S. ⑮ Kamala W. Mei Ling H.	
Notes	10 min — check logs from wknd, check goals	5 min— observe engage ⓞ end of wksp.	10 min — strategy lesson TBD	5 min—	20 min — conf. tbd.

May be photocopied for classroom use. From *The Literacy Teacher's Playbook, Grades 3–6.* Portsmouth, NH: Heinemann. © 2012 by Jennifer Serravallo from *Independent Reading Assessment Fiction.* New York, NY: Scholastic, Inc.

Class Profile

Levels and Goals

NAME	LEVEL	GOAL AND NOTES
Alex A.	O	elaboration (R+W)
Kezia A.	R	engagement + focus (R+W)
Latcesha B.	Q	theme (R/W)
Mei Ling H.	P	vocab/fig lang / word choice
Joana J.	R	secondary char (R)/char development (W)
Vanessa K.	Q	use talk to plan (W)/flex/grow thinking in clubs
Jakson L.	N	retelling longer plots (R)/detailed action (W)
Mark L.	M	inferring-basic traits (R)/show not tell (W)
Caroline M.	M	elaboration (R+W)
Shanique M.	N	inferring traits (show not tell) (W) logical sequence
Mercer N.	R	understanding cause+effect/check for sense (W)
Mateo O.	N	vocab / fig language/word choice (W)
Eliot P.	Q	main char. complexity/create+dev. complex ch. (W)
Nick S.	P	talk w/more elab (R)/write w/elab
Francine S.	R	vocab+fig. lang (R)/Word choice (W)
Rachel S.	O	theme/story has to have deeper meaning
Rajiv T.	R	secondary char analysis/char. dev. (W)
Jasmine V.	N	inferring-basic traits (R)/show not tell
Isabelle W.	V	using symbolism to interpret/plan symbolism
Kamala W.	P	visualizing to stay engaged/increase detail script
Sunniva W.	N	vocab/fig. lang/word choice (W)
Theo Z.	P/Q	stamina in longer books/write w/more det

Figure 4.8 This Class-at-a-Glance Sheet (find a blank version in Appendix C) shows student goals.

◻ Knowing When the Goal Has Been Met

Ideally, this cycle of assessment, goal setting, and teaching will be repeated many times throughout the school year. But when will you know when it's time to go back to the beginning of the cycle, look at fresh work, and set a new goal?

As important as it is to have a clear sense of what you want to work on, you also need to know what it looks like when the work is done. The information in Chapter 2 may be a help to you here. Look back at what made you identify the goal in the first place—probably a gap between the work the student was currently doing and the "ideal" of what that work should look like.

You may also refer to your grade-level standards, rubrics, benchmarks, continuums, and other tools that may provide an image for you of what a strong example of work would be. Some resources for this include:

- *The Continuum of Literacy Learning* (Fountas and Pinnell 2010) offers guidance by Fountas and Pinnell levels of the skills and behaviors students should exhibit.
- *Units of Study in Opinion, Information, and Narrative Writing* (Calkins and colleagues 2013) offers student-facing and teacher-facing checklists of what to look for in information, narrative, and opinion writing, as well as student exemplars.
- *Independent Reading Assessment: Fiction* (Serravallo 2012) and *Independent Reading Assessment: Nonfiction* (Serravallo 2013) contain a ladder of increasing responsibility of student work by reading level, as well as rubrics with sample student responses and descriptors to better understand what it looks like when a student is showing strong comprehension at each level from K–W (fiction) and J–W (nonfiction).

Over the course of the year, a student's goals shift and change. Reading levels increase, and, with that, a student will be tasked with handling a new set of textual challenges. Your curriculum will take you through narrative, informational, and opinion writing units and reading units of study focusing on narrative and informational texts.

A student's strengths and needs, therefore, will evolve as the curriculum and her own development as a reader and writer develop. The teacher's role is to constantly have her eyes open, looking for progress, and knowing when it's time to reestablish a goal. See Figure 4.10 for an example of how Joana's progress—and the monitoring of her progress—evolved across one year. You can keep track of this progress over time with a conferring notes system.

Joana's Goal Setting and Progress Across a School Year

Month	Units of Study in Reading and Writing	Joana's Progress
September	Launching the reading and writing workshops	9/20 Goal established—understanding bigger meanings (What's the point of the story?)
October–November	Character study (reading) and literary essay (writing)	10/30 Showed evidence of goal, new goal established—determining main idea and key details in informational texts; supporting ideas with evidence in essay writing
November–December	Informational reading and informational writing	12/5 Continued with informational reading goals and moved to higher reading level with more complexity—now, multiple main ideas; in writing, moved to multiple paragraphs within each chapter and appropriate support
January	Genre-based book clubs: fantasy and writing fantasy	1/10 In book clubs and in writing partnerships, spoke up and elaborated on thinking
February–March	Reading: interpretation and writing: poetry	2/2 Read closely, paying attention to author's word choice; wrote with careful and surprising word choice
March–April	Test preparation	3/15 Applied the goals from the entire year so far to short test passages in practice and on the day of the test
May–June	Reading: social issue book clubs and writing: social issues	5/25 Deeper exploration of character in reading (secondary characters, character complexity) and in writing to develop more complex characters

Month	Units of Study in Reading and Writing	Joana's Progress
May–June (cont.)		6/20 Established a goal for summer: reading some informational texts in sets with fiction books she's interested in

Figure 4.10 Joana's Goal Setting and Progress Across a School Year

◻ Wrap-Up

As you've worked through this book, I hope that you've been able to internalize the four-step process of collecting data, analyzing it, forming goals, and creating a plan that have the potential to impact your instruction and your students' learning. Working alongside my analysis and goal setting with Joana, I hope that you've kept Alex's work by your side.

At this point, you can turn to your own students' work if you haven't already. Keep in mind, as I mentioned at the end of Chapter 2, that it's unlikely that you'll do this work for every student in your class right away. My hope is that you begin to take on this process with a select handful of students. Maybe those who puzzle you most—your most struggling, your most high-achieving, the student who has been stuck for a while.

As you work to create goals for your students, I hope you've also created goals for yourself. What will you study? What will you read? What will you try?

Keep in mind that this work is never done. The rhythms of this type of data-informed teaching are much like the cycles of the football season. A teaching cycle ends with students reaching their goals; a football season ends (best-case scenario) with the Super Bowl win. After celebrating, training for the next season starts up again. The team moves through training on the field, regular season games, and playoffs—and then on to another Super Bowl. In your classroom, throughout the year, you'll cycle through seasons of monitoring a student's progress, collecting new assessment data, making decisions, crafting a goal, working toward that goal—and, if all goes well, with the student achieving that goal. We're lucky to work in a profession where our learning is never "done": there is always a way to improve one's game, always a way to come up with new plays, new strategies to outgrow your best self—and, with the data on your side, to help your students do the same.

Alex's Work and One Possible Interpretation

Figures A.1–A.6 are available to download at www.heinemann.com/products/E04353.aspx (click on the Companion Resources tab).

Step 1: Collect Data

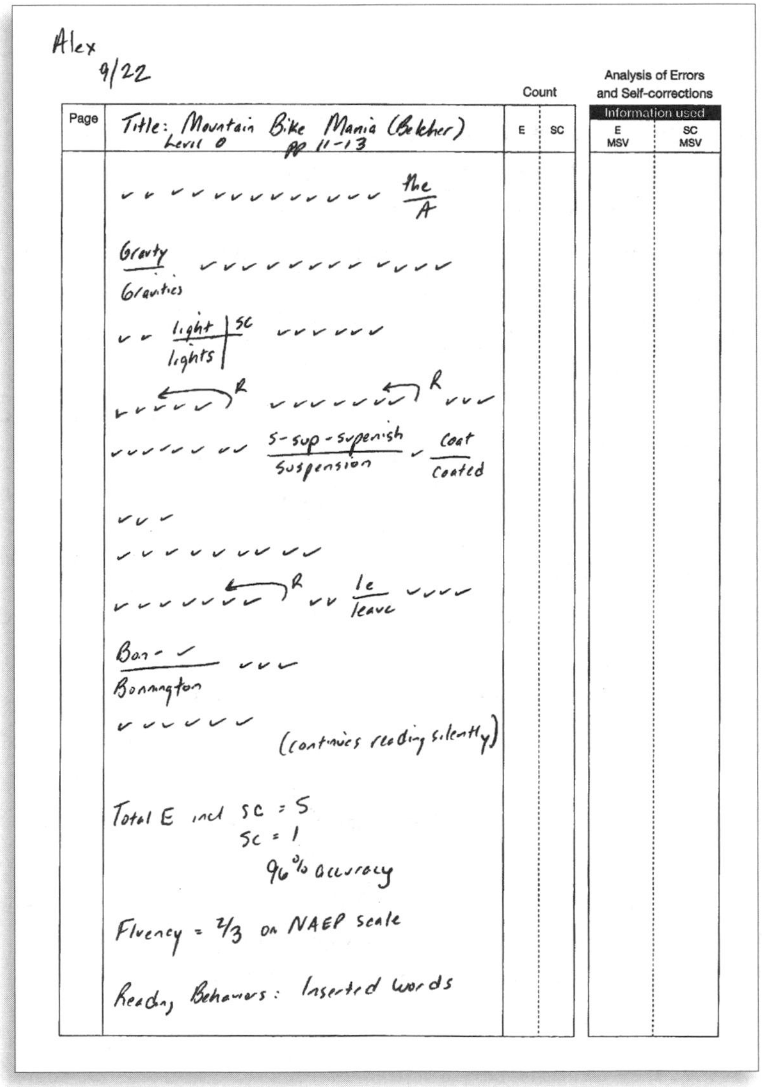

Figure A.1 A running record shows Alex's reading of a level O text. Use this to evaluate fluency, print work, and comprehension. The text excerpt has been provided on page 147 to help you evaluate errors and miscues within sentence context, and to allow you to properly evaluate his retelling and answers to comprehension questions (see page 148).

Running Record Sheet © 2005 by Marie M. Clay from *An Observation Survey of Early Literacy Achievement,* Third Edition (2013). Published by Pearson, a division of Pearson New Zealand Ltd. Reprinted by permission of the author's estate.

Mountain Bike Mania by Angie Belcher

The next morning, on the way to school, Joel and Ocean stopped outside Gravities Edge—the local bike shop. There in the window, gleaming under a dazzle of display lights, was a brand-new mountain bike.

"Wow, Ocean, check it out! I'd give anything to have a cool bike like that with front and back suspension, chrome-coated bars, and rocket sockets!"

"Just looks like a bike to me," she replied.

"If I had one of those, I could leave that Blake "The Brake" Bonnington in my dust. He wouldn't know what hit him!"

For the rest of the week, all Joel could think about was mountain bikes.

Every afternoon, he stopped outside the bike shop and looked longingly in the window.

"Joel, you've got to stop dreaming about that bike and actually do something," Ocean coaxed. "I've got an idea. Why don't we set up a bike-cleaning stand at the track? You can clean off muddy bikes, and I'll sell juice and cups of coffee. I could use Mom's thermos."

"But it would take months to get enough money," Joel sighed. "By that time, it will be gone."

"Well, you think of a better idea then!" Ocean replied.

The next weekend, complete with buckets of soapy water, rags, juice, and coffee, Joel and Ocean set themselves up near the end of the track. Ocean had made a big sign that read: "Treat yourselves—have a drink while we clean your bike!"

Amused by the colorful sign, some of the older riders took advantage of the offer. By the end of the day, the children had cleaned ten bikes.

"Look at all this money, Joel. I guess that's a pretty good start to your bike fund," chirped Ocean brightly.

"Great," grumbled Joel. "I'll only need to clean about a hundred more bikes!"

Retell:

First Joel + Ocean saw bike store w/amazing bike that Joel really wanted. He raised $ so he could get the bike then cleaned bikes and made money. Then he only needed to clean 100 more bikes to get the bike.

Comp Qs:

1. (literal) What did Joel want?
   A cool bike

2. (literal) Why does J. want the bike?
   He could beat Blake.

3. (infer.) What do you think about J & O's relationship?
   She has good ideas to get the bike.

4. (infer.) How is J. feeling @ end? How do you know?
   He feels a little down since he still needs to clean a bit more bikes. He doesn't really need to clean 100, but still a lot more.

Writing About Reading

Figure A.2 A sample of writing about reading from Alex's Book Lover's Book (reading notebook). Use this writing to evaluate Alex's comprehension.

Reading Log

September Reading Log – Due Friday, October 1

Name: Alex   Adult Signature: _____

Date	Home/School	Title	Author	Level	Starting Page	Finishing Page	Minutes Read
9/17	H Ⓢ	Ramonaquimby	B. cleary	0	91	123	40 min
9/17	Ⓗ S	↓ same ↓	same	0	123	131	15 min
9/17	Ⓗ S	↓ same	sa Mc	0	131	47	5 Min = 16 kys
9/18	Ⓗ S	same ↓	same	0	47	65	30 min
9/18	Ⓗ S	↓ same	same	0	65	90	30 min
9/20	H Ⓢ	Otis speford	B. Cleary	0	1	8	12 min
9/20	Ⓗ S	same	↓ samo	0	17	40	30 min 30v.
9/21	H Ⓢ	↓ same ↓	same	0	40	80	30 min
9/21	Ⓗ S	same	same	0	80	92	30 min
9/22	H Ⓢ	↓ same ↓	same	0	92	107	10 min
9/22	H Ⓢ	↓ same	same	0	107	119	30 min
9/22	Ⓗ S	same	same	0	119	35	30 min
9/23	Ⓗ Ⓢ	samy	same	0	135	41	5 min
9/23	Ⓗ S	↓ same ↓	same	0	141	58	30 min
9/24	H Ⓢ	↓ same ↓	same	0	158	173	15 min
9/24	Ⓗ S	↓ same ↓	same	0	173	190	15 min
9/24	Ⓗ S	Gorge's Markelus medic	R. Dahl	0	1	16	5 min
9/24	Ⓗ S	↓ same ↓	R. Dahl	0	16	22	15 min
9/25	Ⓗ S	↓ same	R. Dahl	0	22	34	15 min

Figure A.3 A reading log showing a one-week snapshot of Alex's book selections and reading habits. Use this to evaluate his engagement.

Conversation Transcript

Freckle Juice 5/14

Alex, Shanique, Byron

A: I found a part that was funny (turns to pg w/ post-it).
   It's when Sharon sticks out tongue @ Andrew

S: 1 — Sharon is mean to A. Yc she tricked him

B: Agree — shouldn't drink juice. It's gross! K+M? Yuck!

S: Yes! I would have thrown up! (laughs)

B: why does A. believe her?

S: He just really wants freckles

A: Agree. Must want them really bad to drink that!

S: Mom isn't listening to him.

A: I found another part I like (turns to sticky)
   when he has a dream abt. giant Sharon
   (laughs) she's a monster!

S: I liked that part, too (laughs)

B: Surprised @ end — kid w/ freckles wants them gone.

Figure A.4 A shorthand transcript of Alex's conversation with his partner during reading workshop. Use this to analyze his conversational skills.

Writing Notebook

I herd Gram and
Zadya were selling their
house. I got so sad because
I had so many memorys
in this house. I learn
how to Scouter her. So
I ran to the bath tub
and hide but Melissa
found me and toled
me gram is gonna give
me a supise. So I got
out of the tub and
Gram gave me the
computer. Then, me and
chea play on it all
night.

Figure A.5 A writing notebook entry.
In this sample, Alex attempts to write
a small-moment narrative. Use this to
evaluate qualities of writing, as if it were an
on-demand sample.

Engagement Inventory

Figure A.6

An engagement
inventory showing
Alex's focus,
concentration,
and motivation
during one writer's
workshop period.

Time/Environment:	10–10:15	10:15–10:25	another class (loud out in hall) 10:25–10:35	(phone in room rang) 10:35–11:00		
Names:						
Alex	✓	O / ✓	✓ / O	✓		
Melissa		st		st		
Jenny	✓	✓	✓			
Jose	O	O	✓	O		
Ramon	✓	✓	O	O		
Mark	✓	st	✓	st / ✓		
Desiree	✓	R	✓	R		
Luke		✓	✓			
Shanique	O	✓	✓	O		
Michael	✓	✓	✓			
Joana	✓	✓	✓	O		
Erin	O	O	O	✓		
Isabel	✓	R	R	✓		
Verona	O					
Rebecca	✓	sw	✓	O		
Charlie	✓			O		
David	✓	R	✓	R		
Pete	✓		sw			
Meldwin	O	✓	✓			
Elizabeth	✓	✓	✓	O		
Stella	✓	✓	✓	O		
Luca	✓	✓	✓	✓		
Chloe	✓	✓	✓	✓		

Key:
✓ = engaged   R = reacting (smile / frown)
sw = switch books   O = staring @ me, around room.
st = sticky note

Step 2: Analyze Data

Compare my analysis of each example of Alex's work against your own analysis.

Tool	Strengths	Possibilities for Growth
Running record	• Uses many of the letters in the word (visual cueing system) • Some rereading may indicate monitoring for meaning • Reads in three- or four-word phrase groups • Retelling expresses a beginning, middle, end • Can recall literal details	• Look all the way through the word and cross-check with meaning and syntax. • Read words part by part. • Use monitoring for meaning to self-correct. • Read with more expression/intonation. • Retell the main events that require inference to know what's actually happening. • Elaborate and offer more ideas beyond literal.
Writing about reading	• Reacts to the text • Recalls surprising/interesting parts • Visualizes a character in a setting • Can name character traits and feelings	• Use reactions to have thoughts—elaborate on reactions. • Add more to visualization to include character emotions, actions. • Look at not only the main character but also secondary characters. • Elaborate on why he thinks what he does about the characters (textual evidence).

continues

Tool	Strengths	Possibilities for Growth
Reading log	• Reads within a consistent level • Reading averages around three-quarters of a page per minute • Reads in school and at home each day • Chooses more than one book by the same author	• Read for longer stretches of time (stamina).
Conference transcript and notes	• Is excited about sharing parts of his book • Comes prepared to the conversation with spots in his book marked	• Talk about one idea for a longer stretch of time. • Explain thinking in addition to sharing a favorite part.
Narrative on-demand	• Tells a story in sequence • Chooses a moment of significance • Spells high-frequency words correctly	• Elaborate with details to show, not just tell the character's feelings. • Think about the significance of the moment and try to bring that out in the story. • Spell multisyllabic words part by part.
Engagement inventory—writing	• Has strategies for refocusing himself	• Maintain focus for longer stretches of time.

Step 3: Interpret Data and Establish a Goal

INTERPRETATIONS

I think Alex needs to work on elaboration. In his reading, he gives brief answers to comprehension questions and writes very short responses in his notebook. In writing, his narrative shows only the most basic sketch of a plot.

I believe Alex needs to think more about bigger meaning. In his reading, he mostly recalls literal facts from the story, although he is able to assign some character traits to the main character. In his writing, he tends to write mostly action to the exclusion of other types of details.

I think Alex needs to work on inference and showing, not telling. In his reading, he is just beginning to infer with his work around naming character traits, but he could do more work to understand when something should have a literal versus figurative meaning. In his writing, he tells how a character's feeling, but he could work to show not just what's happening but how it's happening.

I think Alex needs to work on stamina in reading and writing. His narratives are short and his engagement during writing workshop is spotty. In looking at his reading log, he often reads for short bursts and needs to learn to read for longer stretches.

I think Alex needs to work on decoding and encoding. In his writing sample, he tends to spell many words incorrectly, not always relying on words he knows or syllabication to help him spell new words (i.e., scouter instead of scooter and supise instead of surprise). In reading, when coming upon an unfamiliar word he tends to read letter by letter, not word part by word part (i.e., Gravty instead of Grav-i-ties or Supenish instead of sus-pen-sion).

GOAL

Of these four, I am going to choose *elaboration*. I think that teaching Alex ways to say more and think more would naturally mean that he's not just thinking literally but also inferentially. I also think that teaching him ways to extend his reading and writing time, and his thinking during reading and writing, will help improve his stamina and time on task. Maybe his lack of stamina is a result of him not knowing what else he could be doing.

Step 4: Develop an Action Plan

STRATEGIES

- Reading: Using reading notebook, have Alex keep track of important events and his responses to the events. On the left side, he should record what's happening. On the right side, he should record what he thinks about what's happening.
- Reading: What and why. Suggest that Alex think not just about what's happened, but why it might have happened. When he finds himself reacting to a spot in the text, he could record the why on a sticky note.
- Reading: Alex could try reading at a lower level to see if it's easier to say more about the text. Level O seems like a stretch where maybe only basic thinking is happening.
- Reading: Utilize partnership time for his partner to get Alex to elaborate more using the same strategies he's practicing independently.
- Writing: Have Alex try to write partner sentences for each sentence he wrote. He could cut apart the draft to give space within and among the details that are already there. Have him add in any extra detail—dialogue, action, thinking, setting—to try to say more.
- Writing: After a first draft, suggest Alex draw a sketch with details of who is in the scene, where it's happening, and what's happening. He could go back to the draft to see if there are details in the sketch that he can add to the words.
- Writing: Utilize partnership time for his partner to get him to elaborate using the same strategies he's practicing independently.

METHODS

- Small-group strategy lessons—Introduce the strategies mentioned previously in small groups with other students who need similar support.
- Conferences—Check in with Alex one-on-one when possible.
- Partnership—Although formal partnerships aren't yet established, supply his partner with a list of prompts to help draw more information out of him (for example, "What makes you think that?" or "What do you think about that?").

TEACHING OVER TIME

- Try to see Alex in small group at least twice a week in reading and twice in writing.
- Involve his speech and language teacher in this goal. Try to get the teacher to help Alex practice saying more when storytelling out loud, and send his writing folder with him during pullout intervention so that he can apply what he's practicing aloud in his writing.

KNOWING WHEN THE GOAL HAS BEEN MET

- Reading—Have Alex read for thirty to forty minutes at an appropriate pace (three-quarters of a page per minute).
- Writing—Double the length of his written responses to reading, and double the length of his narrative writing.
- Talk—Increase the amount of time he is able to talk about one topic with his partner.

APPENDIX B
Glossary of Assessment Terms

In a data-driven educational climate, buzzwords abound. The days of getting by without hearing words like *formative, summative, universal screening,* and *progress monitoring* are in the past. We're all working to catch on quickly and make changes to our teaching practices so that we're aligned with the needs of today's classroom. Learning the meaning of these terms might help you assign language to some of what you already do and might help you identify areas that you've yet to explore. But the purpose of this book is to do more than just impress your friends at a dinner party with your edu-savvy vocabulary.

In this appendix, you'll learn some of the important aspects of assessment. Use the information to help you reflect on the assessments you use to get information about your readers and writers. See if there is a balance of the types of assessment you use and how you use them. If you discover there are types of assessments you aren't currently in the habit of using but would like to, I provide examples that are elaborated on in Chapter One.

Formative vs. Summative Assessment

Formative assessment is part of the instructional process. Formative assessments are collected and analyzed on the go and help teachers get information to both plan and modify instruction. Ideally, students are involved in reflecting on formative assessment. Teachers might help students by providing exemplars and/or benchmarks and guiding students in reflecting about their own work in comparison to the sample work.

Formative assessments are frequent and provide ongoing feedback to teachers and students about where students are in their learning journey. In this sense, formative assessment informs both teachers and students about student understanding at a point when timely adjustments can be made. Formative assessments typically aren't "graded."

Here are some examples of assessments that could be considered formative:

- book logs
- stop-and-jot writing in the midst of reading
- reading reflection
- on-demand writing sample

Summative assessments are given periodically to determine what students know and understand at a particular point in time. Sometimes summative assessments are given at the end of a unit of study or at predetermined time frames across the year. Many associate summative assessments only with standardized tests such as state assessments, but they can also be used to inform work within the classroom. Summative assessment at the district/classroom level is an accountability measure that is generally used as part of the grading process (Garrison and Ehringhaus 2007). Here are some examples of the types of assessments that could be considered summative assessments:

- state assessments
- district benchmark or interim assessments, such as running records (Directed Reading Assessment or the like)
- end-of-unit assessments
- published writing from an entire unit of study

Formal vs. Informal Assessments

Formal assessments are typically standardized. To be considered formal or standardized, they have been field-tested on students and have sometimes undergone some type of study by a scientist who studies testing, called a *psychometrician*. They have been deemed valid and reliable. *Valid* means that the assessment actually assesses what it says it does. *Reliable* means that if the same student were to take the same test more than once, the results would be comparable. The results of formal assessments are often reported as statistics, percentiles, or stanines—numbers. Some examples of formal assessments are:

- the Directed Reading Assessment
- state standardized tests
- college entrance exams such as the Scholastic Aptitude Test (SAT)
- IQ tests such as the Stanford-Binet

Informal assessments are often content and performance driven. Teachers may create tools to evaluate informal assessments, such as rubrics or checklists. Really any artifact that shows a student's learning or understanding could be considered an informal assessment. Results from an informal assessment are usually kept within the classroom and are not reported elsewhere. Examples of informal assessments may include:

- end-of-unit assessments
- a transcript of a student conversation

- an on-demand quick write in response to a prompt during a read-aloud
- a student's writing notebook sample

Qualitative vs. Quantitative

Quantitative refers to numbers. Any type of assessment that yields a score, a number, a letter, or a percentage can be considered quantitative. Quantitative measures are erroneously what people typically think of when they use the word *data*. Often, quantitative data are valued over qualitative data by policy makers because it's easier to create graphs and charts, disaggregate the data, and perform statistical analyses on the data. However, for the purposes of guiding classroom instruction, it's important that a teacher has qualitative data as well. Quantitative data include:

- reading levels
- standardized test score
- reading rate (words/minute)

Qualitative measures attempt to provide descriptions of what is happening with the student, usually in words. Qualitative measures often allow teachers to be more nuanced and descriptive and offer more insight into not only the results, but also the why behind results. Examples include:

- a summary of the types of work a student has done over the course of a semester
- a student's written reflection on how he's accomplished his goal
- anecdotal records on a student's work during conferences

Universal Screening

Universal screening takes place approximately three times across a school year. The purpose is to screen for, and identify, students whose reading achievement is significantly below what is expected so that a plan can be made for them to receive additional support. Universal screening has become particularly popular with the advent of Response to Intervention (RTI) initiatives.

If your school is deciding upon a universal screening tool, be aware that the best tools give a broad scope of "reading achievement." By contrast, tools such as Dynamic Indicators of Basic Early Literacy Skills (DIBELS) narrowly define what it means to read and don't offer helpful information about what to do once you've determined a child is in need of intervention (Goodman 2006; Pearson 2006). Universal screening tools that may more accurately reflect literacy practices you value and you're looking to support may include:

- *Benchmark Assessment System (BAS)* (Fountas and Pinnell 2010)
- *Qualitative Reading Inventory—5* (Leslie and Caldwell 2010)
- *Analytical Reading Inventory* (Woods and Moe 2010)

ACTION ⟶

Spread the student work examples you've collected, or Alex's, on the table in front of you. With a sticky note, use the terms in this section to label each artifact. Keep in mind that each artifact can fit into more than one category. For example, something can be both qualitative and formative.

⬚ Progress Monitoring

Progress monitoring is a term used within an RTI framework that involves collecting repeated measures of performance to "(a) estimate rates of improvement, (b) identify students who are not demonstrating adequate progress, and/or (c) compare the efficacy of different forms of instruction to design more effective, individualized instruction" (National Center on Response to Intervention 2009).

Teachers can create their own tools or use tools available on the professional market (see www.rti4success.org or www.rtinetwork.org for more information). What's important is that any one type of assessment—say, oral reading rate—is not the only measure of performance considered. As already discussed, overreliance on one area of reading will give a warped perspective of the whole and may mislead a teacher to focus on an area of the child's reading that will not yield the desired progress (German and Newman 2007).

APPENDIX C

Forms Reproducible forms are available to download at www.heinemann.com/products/E04353.aspx (click on the Companion Resources tab).

Table for Summarizing Analysis of Data

Tool	Strengths	Possibilities for Growth
Reading Log	•	•
Writing about Reading	•	•
Running Record	•	•
Independent Reading Assessment	•	•

Possible Goals

I think _____ needs to _____

because I saw _____ when looking at the

_____, and _____

when looking at the _____.

I think _____ needs to _____

because I saw _____ when looking at the

_____, and _____

when looking at the _____.

I think _____ needs to _____

because I saw _____ when looking at the

_____, and _____

when looking at the _____.

I think _____ needs to _____

because I saw _____ when looking at the

_____, and _____

when looking at the _____.

Class Profile

Levels and Goals		
NAME	**LEVEL**	**GOAL AND NOTES**

Planning Your Week

	Monday	Tuesday	Wednesday	Thursday	Friday
Strategy Lesson (10 min)					
Strategy Lesson (10 min)					
Conferences (5 minutes each)					
Guided Reading (15–20 min)					
Other (_____ min)					
Notes					

Home–School Communication Letter

Dear _____,

_____ and I have recently had a conversation to set goals for the coming weeks of reading and writing. Goals help us to have a focus and intention when practicing reading and writing at home and at school. We wanted to let you know about our conversation so that you can provide support as well.

Reading Goal:	**Writing Goal:**

We expect that with daily practice, the goals will be accomplished on or around _____.

Here are some ways you can help _____ at home:

Reading	**Writing**

I welcome your thoughts and feedback!

Sincerely,

Note-Taking Form to Communicate with Other Teachers

Who	Date	Strengths	Teaching Possibilities

Works Cited

Adler, David A. Various dates. Cam Jansen series. New York, NY: Puffin.

Afflerbach, Peter, P. David Pearson, and Scott G. Paris. 2008. "Clarifying Differences Between Reading Skills and Reading Strategies." *The Reading Teacher* 61 (5): 364–373.

Allington, Richard L. 2011. *What Really Matters for Struggling Readers: Designing Research-Based Programs*. 3d ed. New York, NY: Pearson.

Anderson, Carl. 2000. *How's It Going? A Practical Guide to Conferring with Student Writers*. Portsmouth, NH: Heinemann.

———. 2005. *Assessing Writers*. Portsmouth, NH: Heinemann.

Bear, Donald R., Marcia R. Invernizzi, Shane Templeton, and Francine R. Johnston. 2011. *Words Their Way: Word Study for Phonics, Vocabulary, and Spelling Instruction*. 5th ed. New York, NY: Pearson.

Beers, Kylene, and Robert E. Probst. 2012. *Notice and Note: Strategies for Close Reading*. Portsmouth, NH: Heinemann.

Boelts, Maribeth. 2009. *Those Shoes*. Somerville, MA: Candlewick Press.

Bomer, Randy, and Katherine Bomer. 2001. *For a Better World: Reading and Writing for Social Action*. Portsmouth, NH: Heinemann.

Calkins, Lucy McCormick. 2000. *The Art of Teaching Reading*. New York, NY: Pearson.

Calkins, Lucy, Amanda Hartman, and Zoë Ryder White. 2005. *One to One: The Art of Conferring with Young Writers*. Portsmouth, NH: Heinemann.

Calkins, Lucy, Kathleen Tolan, and Mary Ehrenworth. 2010. *Units of Study for Teaching Reading, Grades 3–5: A Curriculum for the Reading Workshop*. Portsmouth, NH: Heinemann.

Calkins, Lucy, with Colleagues from the Reading and Writing Project. 2011. *Curricular Plans for the Reading and Writing Workshop, Grades K–8*. Portsmouth, NH: Heinemann.

———. 2013. *Units of Study in Opinion, Information, and Narrative Writing: A Common Core Workshop Curriculum*. Portsmouth, NH: Heinemann.

Clay, Marie. 1991. *Becoming Literate*. Portsmouth, NH: Heinemann.

———. 2000. *Running Records for Classroom Teachers*. Portsmouth, NH: Heinemann.

Coerr, Eleanor. 2004. *Sadako and the Thousand Paper Cranes*. New York, NY: Puffin Books.

Cruz, M. Colleen. 2004. *Independent Writing: One Teacher—Thirty-Two Needs, Topics, and Plans*. Portsmouth, NH: Heinemann.

———. 2008. *A Quick Guide to Reaching Struggling Writers, K–5*. Portsmouth, NH: Heinemann.

Culham, Ruth. 2008. *6 + 1 Traits of Writing: The Complete Guide, Grades 3 and Up*. New York, NY: Scholastic.

Daniels, Harvey. 2002. *Literature Circles: Voice and Choice in Book Clubs and Reading Groups*. Portland, ME: Stenhouse Publishers.

Duffy, G. G., et al. 1987. "Effects of Explaining the Reasoning Associated with Using Reading Strategies." *Reading Research Quarterly* 22: 347–38.

Ehrenworth, Mary, and Vicki Vinton. 2005. *The Power of Grammar: Unconventional Approaches to the Conventions of Language*. Portsmouth, NH: Heinemann.

Elkind, David. 1976. *Child Development and Education: A Piagetian Perspective*. New York, NY: Oxford University Press.

Ericsson, K. Anders, Ralf Th. Krampe, and Clemens Tesch-Römer. 1993. "The Role of Deliberate Practice in the Acquisition of Expert Performance." *Psychological Review* 100 (3): 363–406.

Feigelson, Daniel. 2008. *Practical Punctuation: Lessons on Rule Making and Rule Breaking in Elementary Writing*. Portsmouth, NH: Heinemann.

Fisher, Douglas, and Nancy Frey. 2008. *Better Learning through Structured Teaching: A Framework for the Gradual Release of Responsibility*. Alexandria, VA: Association for Supervision and Curriculum Development.

Fisher, Douglas, Nancy Frey, and Diane Lapp. 2012. *Text Complexity: Raising Rigor in Reading*. Newark, DE: International Reading Association.

Fletcher, Ralph. 2006. *Boy Writers: Reclaiming Their Voices*. Portland, ME: Stenhouse Publishers.

Fountas, Irene C., and Gay Su Pinnell. 1996. *Guided Reading: Good First Teaching for All Children*. Portsmouth, NH: Heinemann.

———. 2006. *Teaching for Comprehending and Fluency. Thinking, Talking, and Writing About Reading, K–8*. Portsmouth, NH: Heinemann.

———. 2008. *When Readers Struggle: Teaching That Works*. Portsmouth, NH: Heinemann.

———. 2010. *The Continuum of Literacy Learning, Grades PreK–8*, Second Edition. Portsmouth, NH: Heinemann.

———. 2011. *Benchmark Assessment System*. 2d ed. Portsmouth, NH: Heinemann.

Garrison, Catherine, and Michael Ehringhaus. 2007. "Formative and Summative Assessments in the Classroom." Retrieved from www.amle.org/publications/webexclusive/assessment/tabid/1120/default.aspx.

German, Diane J., and Rochelle S. Newman. 2007. "Oral Reading Skills of Children with Oral Language (Word-Finding) Difficulties." *Reading Psychology* 28 (5): 397–442.

Gladwell, Malcolm. 2002. *The Tipping Point: How Little Things Can Make a Big Difference*. New York, NY: Back Bay Books.

Goodman, Kenneth S. 2006. "A Critical Review of DIBELS." In *The Truth About DIBELS: What It Is—What It Does*, ed. Kenneth S. Goodman, 1–39. Portsmouth, NH: Heinemann.

Guthrie, John T., and Allan Wigfield. 1997. *Reading Engagement: Motivating Readers Through Integrated Instruction*. Newark, DE: International Reading Association.

Harvey, Stephanie, and Anne Goudvis. 2007. *Strategies That Work: Teaching Comprehension for Understanding and Engagement*. 2d ed. Portland, ME: Stenhouse Publishers.

Hattie, John. 1999. "Influences on Student Learning." Available from www.arts.auckland.ac.nz/staff/index. cfm?P=5049.

Johnston, Peter H. 2004. *Choice Words: How Our Language Affects Children's Learning*. Portland, ME: Stenhouse Publishers.

Keene, Ellin Oliver. 2006. *Assessing Comprehension Thinking Strategies*. Huntington Beach, CA: Shell Education.

———. 2008. *To Understand: New Horizons in Reading Comprehension*. Portsmouth, NH: Heinemann.

Keene, Ellin Oliver, and Susan Zimmermann. 2007. *Mosaic of Thought: The Power of Comprehension Strategy Instruction*. 2d ed. Portsmouth, NH: Heinemann.

Keene, Ellin Oliver, et al. 2011. *Comprehension Going Forward: Where We Are / What's Next*. Portsmouth, NH: Heinemann.

Koch, Richard. 2008. *The 80/20 Principle: The Secret of Achieving More with Less*. 2d ed. New York, NY: Doubleday.

Kuhn, Melanie R. 2008. *The Hows and Whys of Fluency Instruction*. New York, NY: Pearson.

Lehman, Christopher. 2011. *A Quick Guide to Reviving Disengaged Writers, 5–8*. Portsmouth, NH: Heinemann.

Lehman, Christopher, and Kate Roberts. 2013. *Falling in Love with Close Reading: Lessons for Analyzing Texts—and Life*. Portsmouth, NH: Heinemann.

Leslie, Lauren, and JoAnne Schudt Caldwell. 2010. *Qualitative Reading Inventory—5*. Upper Saddle River, NJ: Pearson.

Lobel, Arnold. Various dates. Frog and Toad series. New York, NY: HarperCollins.

Miller, Donalyn. 2009. *The Book Whisperer: Awakening the Inner Reader in Every Child*. San Francisco, CA: Jossey-Bass.

National Center on Response to Intervention. 2009. Available from http://www.rti4success.org/categorycontents/progress_monitoring

Nichols, Maria. 2006. *Comprehension Through Conversation: The Power of Purposeful Talk in the Reading Workshop*. Portsmouth, NH: Heinemann.

Paris, Scott G., David R. Cross, and Marjorie Y. Lipson. 1984. "Informed Strategies for Learning: A Program to Improve Children's Reading Awareness and Comprehension." *Journal of Educational Psychology* (76) 1239–1252.

Park, Barbara. 1988. *The Kid in the Red Jacket*. New York, NY: Yearling Books.

Pearson, P. David. 2006. Foreword to *The Truth About DIBELS*, ed. Kenneth S. Goodman, v–xxiv. Portsmouth, NH: Heinemann.

Pearson, P. David, and Margaret C. Gallagher. 1983. "The Instruction of Reading Comprehension." *Contemporary Educational Psychology* (8): 317–344.

Pearson, P. David, Laura R. Roehler, Janice A. Dole, and Gerald G. Duffy. 1992. "Developing Expertise in Reading Comprehension." In *What Research Has to Say About Reading Instruction*. 2d ed. Eds. S. Jay Samuels and Alan E. Farstrup, 145–199. Newark, DE: International Reading Association.

Petty, Geoffrey. 2006. *Evidence Based Teaching: A Practical Approach.* Cheltenham, UK: Nelson Thornes.

Philbrick, Rodman. 2001. *Freak the Mighty.* New York, NY: Scholastic.

Pink, Daniel H. 2011. *Drive: The Surprising Truth About What Motivates Us.* New ed. New York, NY: Riverhead Books.

Rasinski, Timothy. 2010. *The Fluent Reader: Oral & Silent Reading Strategies for Building Fluency, Word Recognition & Comprehension.* 2d ed. New York, NY: Scholastic.

Riordan, Rick. 2010. *The Lightning Thief.* New York, NY: Hyperion Books

Rosenblatt, Louise M. 1994. *The Reader, The Text, The Poem: The Transactional Theory of the Literary Work.* Carbondale, IL: Southern Illinois University Press.

Rylant, Cynthia. 2006. *The Van Gogh Café.* Boston, MA: HMH Books for Young Readers.

Sachar, Louis. 1988. *There's a Boy in the Girl's Bathroom.* New York, NY: Yearling Books.

Serravallo, Jennifer. 2010. *Teaching Reading in Small Groups: Differentiated Instruction for Building Strategic, Independent Readers.* Portsmouth, NH: Heinemann.

———. 2012. *Independent Reading Assessment: Fiction, Grade 3.* New York, NY: Scholastic.

———. 2012. *Independent Reading Assessment: Fiction, Grade 4.* New York, NY: Scholastic.

———. 2012. *Independent Reading Assessment: Fiction, Grade 5.* New York, NY: Scholastic.

———. 2013. *Independent Reading Assessment: Nonfiction, Grade 3.* New York, NY: Scholastic.

———. 2013. *Independent Reading Assessment: Nonfiction, Grade 4.* New York, NY: Scholastic.

———. 2013. *Independent Reading Assessment: Nonfiction, Grade 5.* New York, NY: Scholastic.

———. 2014. *The Literacy Teacher's Playbook, Grades K–2: Four Steps for Turning Assessment Data into Goal-Directed Instruction.* Portsmouth, NH: Heinemann.

Serravallo, Jennifer, and Gravity Goldberg. 2007. *Conferring with Readers: Supporting Each Student's Growth and Independence*. Portsmouth, NH: Heinemann.

Smith, Michael W., and Jeffrey D. Wilhelm. 2006. *Going with the Flow: How to Engage Boys (and Girls) in their Literacy Learning*. Portsmouth, NH: Heinemann.

Spinelli, Jerry. 1999. *Maniac Magee*. New York, NY: Little, Brown Books for Young Readers.

Sulzby, Elizabeth. 1994. "Children's Emergent Reading of Favorite Storybooks." In *Theoretical Models and Processes of Reading*. 4th ed. Eds. R. B. Ruddell, M. R. Ruddell, and H. Singer, 244–280. Newark, DE: International Reading Association.

Truss, Lynne. 2006. *Eats, Shoots & Leaves: The Zero Tolerance Approach to Punctuation*. New York, NY: Gotham Books.

Vygotsky, Lev. 1978. "Interaction Between Learning and Development." In *Mind In Society: The Development of Higher Psychological Processes*. Cambridge, MA: Harvard University Press.

Wiggins, Grant. 2013. "On So-Called 'Reading Strategies'—The Utter Mess that is the Literature and Advice to Teachers." Available at http://grantwiggins.wordpress.com/2013/03/04/on-so-called-reading-strategies-the-utter-mess-that-is-the-literature-and-advice-to-teachers/. Last accessed June 19, 2013.

Wood, David, Jerome S. Bruner, and Gail Ross. 1976. The Role of Tutoring in Problem Solving. *Journal of Child Psychology and Psychiatry* 17 (2): 89 100.

Woods, Mary Lynn, and Alden J. Moe. 2010. *Analytical Reading Inventory: Comprehensive Standards-Based Assessment for all Students Including Gifted and Remedial*. 9th ed.

Zimmermann, Susan, and Chryse Hutchins. 2003. *7 Keys to Comprehension: How to Help Your Kids Read It and Get It!* New York, NY: Three Rivers Press.